Buddhism

&

The Twelve Steps

Also by Kevin Griffin:

One Breath at a Time: Buddhism and the Twelve Steps, Rodale Press, 2004

A Burning Desire: Dharma God and the Path of Recovery, Hay House, 2010

Laughing Buddha, Music CD, One Breath Records, 2013

Buddhism

&

The Twelve Steps

A Recovery Workbook

for

Individuals and Groups

By Kevin Griffin

Notice: This book is intended as a reference volume only, not as a medical manual. Addiction can be a serious disease with implications beyond the scope of this book. If you believe you have a problem, please seek out the best medical and therapeutic advice available.

Pre-emptive Apology

I worked on this book sporadically over several years. I am the author, editor, copy-editor, designer, and publisher. Therefore it is probably more flawed than the typical book from a large publishing company. I hope you will forgive any gaps, redundancies, typos, and other errors. If you find something egregious that you feel needs correcting, please contact me through my website, www.kevingriffin.net.

Thank you,

Kevin Griffin

Praise for *Buddhism & The Twelve Steps*

"A wonderful and refreshingly practical resource for integrating mindfulness practices into 12-step recovery." - **Sarah Bowen**, PhD, co-author of *Mindfulness-Based Relapse Prevention for Addictive Behaviors.*

"*Buddhism & The Twelve Steps* offers practical and effective exercises that will assist the reader in developing and enhancing a fulfilling Buddhist practice." – **Roland Williams**, President and CEO Free Life Enterprises and VIP Recovery Coaching

"An excellent tool for recovering the happiness, joy, and freedom that life offers each of us if we are only willing to go for it." – **Lee McCormick**, CEO Integrative Life Center, author of *The Spirit Recovery Meditation Journal.*

Praise for *One Breath at a Time*

"The shared message of the possibility of freedom rings clearly from every page." - **Sylvia Boorstein**, author of *Pay Attention, For Goodness' Sake: The Buddhist Path of Kindness*

"A brilliant merging of Buddhist insights with those of the Twelve Step program." - **Wes Nisker**, author of *The Essential Crazy Wisdom, Buddha's Nature,* and *The Big Bang, the Buddha, and the Baby Boom*

"a valuable book," ***Publishers Weekly***

"powerful and affecting," ***Library Journal***

Praise for *A Burning Desire*

"A truly helpful bridge between the power of 12 step work and the power of the Dharma." - **Jack Kornfield**, author of *The Wise Heart*.

"Promises to be the seminal text for the recovery community of the 21st century!" - **William Alexander**, story teller, and author of *Cool Water: Alcoholism, Mindfulness and Ordinary Recovery*

"Kevin is a master at building bridges between the 12 Steps and Buddhism. I highly recommend this book to anyone in recovery that is interested in Buddhism!" - **Noah Levine** author of *Dharma Punx* and *Against the Stream*

"A landmark book in the path of recovery." - **G. Alan Marlatt**, Ph.D., author of *Relapse Prevention* and *Assessment of Addictive Behaviors*

Dedication

For all those who are doing the work of recovery.

Table of Contents

Preface

This book is something of an accident, having come out of conversations with an editor who thought he'd like to publish it and with a friend who told me that people liked reading my books but didn't know what they were supposed to *do*.

So, I began to put down my ideas, first writing about mindfulness practice and its relationship to recovery, then going through the 12 Steps. What I found myself doing was "reverse engineering" my own program. I asked myself how I went about working the Steps and dealing with the challenges of life and a meditation practice. What became apparent to me is that my approach to recovery, healing, and spiritual growth is more intuitive than systematic, more like stumbling around in the dark trying to find my way than following a structured path or program. And, truth be told, that's what I think this process is for most of us. It's nice to have someone present you with a package that claims to be "the way," because it makes you feel safe and gives your mind something to hold on to. But I don't think recovery really works like that. I don't think there is a step-by-step, fill-in-the-blanks, one-size-fits-all program (despite my commitment to the 12 Steps). I think we all have to find our own way. Yes, there are some great road signs along the way, some well-traveled paths we can try out, and in the beginning of recovery, when you really have no idea what you're doing, it's smart to just stick to the basics and the guidelines and advice of those more experienced than you. But pretty soon you're going to have to make this your own, because if you try to maintain your recovery based on someone else's program, eventually it's not going to work and you'll be stuck.

Lots of people run into this problem. At five years or ten years or twenty years into recovery they realize that their program is hollow. They've been showing up and doing all the things their sponsor or their 12 Step literature told them to, but now they realize that they've never internalized the process, that they don't feel any real connection—whether to "Higher Power," or more generally to a spiritual way of living, or simply to their own heart. They want more, a genuine spiritual experience, not just a "fake it till you make it" version of recovery, or even the outer trappings of success in a program—a job, a relationship, kids, or whatever their definition of success is. They want something real, something that feels like their own.

Of course, I was never one to follow the rules, anyway. I quit high school and became a musician; when I got sober twenty years later I had never been married or had kids, had no insurance of any kind, didn't own anything other than my guitars and my clothes, and had recently opened my first bank account. So, getting sober was about learning how to live more conventionally, how to follow the rules. I worked the Steps with a sponsor, got a day job, went back to school and eventually got married and became a father—and now I've got loads of insurance and at least enough money in the bank to pay the bills. But way back there, around five or six years sober (over twenty years ago), the internal process of recovery started to change. I still went (and go) to meetings, but my idea and understanding of "How It Works" (a famous chapter title in AA) has changed significantly.

So, I guess you could say that this book is *my* "How It Works," or at least, how it works for me. I don't expect you to benefit from all the ideas and exercises here. That's not the point. What I do hope is that some of the elements of my approach to recovery will act as inspirations to you to find your own way and understanding of your recovery process.

One note: I use the terms "alcoholic" and "addict," somewhat interchangeably. An alcoholic is basically an alcohol addict. I also mean the term addict to actually refer to anyone who might be in a 12 Step program, including co-dependents, adult children of alcoholics, or anyone else. I personally identify as an alcoholic and addict, as drinking and smoking pot were my primary problems. But I have symptoms of various other addictions.

Introduction

What does it mean to "work the Steps"? The phrase is tossed around at meetings and between people in recovery as though everyone knows what it means. But working the Steps isn't like building a house or learning to drive. There are no blueprints or rules of the road. Okay, that's not true. People have written blueprints, but I'm not convinced that any of them are the definitive way to work the Steps.

For a lot of people, the phrase probably means something like going through one of those workbooks that give you loads of questions to answer about every Step. You go through it, fill out the blank pages, and, poof, you're cured!

Not so fast.

I can't say a lot about these kinds of books since I've never worked through one. When I start to read the questions, I get annoyed or bored.

The thing is, I didn't get a sponsor till I was already a year clean and sober, and one of the first things he said to me was, "If you made it through a year you must have worked the first three Steps, so let's start on Step Four." Which means I never worked Steps One to Three with a sponsor. I know a lot of people write their Step One, reviewing all the behaviors and consequences of their addiction. Although I didn't do that in a written way, I did reflect on it repeatedly. This reflection convinced me that I could never go back to drinking and using because it simply didn't work. I'd tried for years to control and enjoy drugs and alcohol, and I couldn't. Step One helped me to finally see and accept this once and for all. Done.

Steps Two and Three were more internal and ongoing—Step Three still is. I formally did Steps Four through Nine with my sponsor, writing the inventory, reading it to him, doing the prayers in the AA Big Book, making the list and making amends. That's the closest I've come to officially working the Steps. But I by no means believe that going through those six Steps once was all I needed to do with them. What I learned in that process and adopted as a way of living in and viewing the world has informed my life ever since.

So, yes I went through a process that could be called "working the Steps"--at least some of them—but I don't believe that this one-time effort in any way fulfilled my recovery work. For me, the term doesn't really fit the process. I think it's more important to "live the Steps" than to work them. We have to integrate the values and principles of the Steps into our lives if they are to mean anything beyond detox and getting sober for a little while. Living the Steps has wide-ranging implications, touching every part of our lives. But for me, the starting point is always inside, and that's why meditation is the cornerstone of my program.

Today, rather than writing the Steps, I use meditation as the tool for working the Steps. Let me give you an idea of how that works:

When I sit down to meditate I come face-to-face with my lack of control over my body and mind, thus seeing that I am powerless—Step One.

I meditate because I believe that the benefits derived from this work, those qualities that are developed and the insights that are revealed can bring harmony and clarity to my life—Step Two.

When I meditate I turn myself over to a process that is beyond my control. I don't control the results of my practice, but I do invariably benefit from it—Step Three.

During meditation all my stuff comes up. You could call this Step Ten rather than Step Four because it's more concerned with what's happening right now than my history. But in any case, meditation reveals my inventory.

Since Step Five involves another person. I can't fully do it alone, so this is one Step I can't do in solitary meditation. Nonetheless, the "admitted to God" and "to ourselves" parts are done in meditation.

Meditation is the groundwork for letting go—Step Six.

In meditation, I let go—Step Seven.

In meditation those I've harmed appear in my mind, especially in formal lovingkindness practice—Step Eight.

Although I can't make amends to others in a traditional way through meditation, I can offer them love and compassion. But the more significant way I relate Step Nine to meditation is as an amends to myself, a healing practice.

Step Ten, see Step Four.

Step Eleven is the place where we're encouraged to meditate, so the connection is direct.

Through the process of meditation and Buddhist practice, just as with the Steps, there are insights and openings that can be called "spiritual awakening," Step Twelve. In fact, I think it's difficult to have a transformative awakening without some form of meditative or contemplative work.

How to Use This Book

The purpose of this book is to give you practical tools for working with your recovery and with the Twelve Steps, all based on Buddhist teachings, practices, and principles. The heart of the book is the exercises. I've used many of these in my workshops and retreats, as well as in my own program and practice for many years. Some I made up as I was writing the book. Frankly, you can make up your own. That's because, what's important isn't my particular approach to this process, but that *you* become engaged in the process. I'm only trying to help you with that, not control how you go about it.

There are two broad categories of exercises: group and individual. Many exercises can be used in either way, while others are specifically designed for one or the other. While the group exercises are mostly meant to be topics discussed in dyads or small groups, the individual exercises take many forms.

Contemplative: some exercises take quiet reflection. Contemplation is when we take a question or an idea and keep going over it, approaching it from different directions and trying to dig for deeper layers of understanding and insight.

Meditative: there are many meditation exercises which are trying to help you train the mind to be more present and calm, to develop insight, and open the heart. These will usually be done in silence after you've read the instructions.

Written: some of the exercises are designed to be written out. Writing forces us to make cogent and coherent what might only be unstructured, inchoate ideas in the mind. When we have to make sentences and paragraphs out of those ideas, we often learn a lot.

Blended: many times I will suggest that you meditate before doing a written or contemplative exercise. This allows you to clear the mind and deepen your ability to think.

Daily exercises: many of the exercises are meant to be brought into your daily life, both as behaviors and awareness exercises. Ultimately we are trying to change our lives, so the exercises should be relevant to our lives.

The Path

Both Buddhism and the Twelve Steps present our spiritual journey as a process, a movement from pain and confusion to happiness and wisdom. The process they describe is not, I think, unique to either of them, but reflects each tradition's attempt to solve the human riddle of suffering. As such, I think that they each tap into something deeper than the forms, language, cultural trappings, and historical context from which they spring. I believe that they each express something archetypal, a path deeply embedded in human consciousness that has been explored by seekers since humans awakened to their own mortality.

Joseph Campbell called this path "The Hero's Journey," and traditionally it starts in darkness, takes the seeker through trials where he or she has to face both inner and outer demons, and resolves itself with some kind of actual or metaphorical homecoming. Certainly this describes the addict's recovery process where we come out of the darkness of compulsion and humiliating dependence into a realization of our problem; this realization is followed by a spiritual surrender and psychological house cleaning.

Amends for our mistakes follow, and finally we try to pass on our hard-earned wisdom. The Buddhist version of this process involves seeing suffering in ourselves and others, letting go of its causes, surrendering to the truth, and cultivating the path of freedom.

Fundamentally, each of these versions of the path is founded in honesty and acknowledging what is true. As long as we live in our illusions, both about ourselves and about the world, we have no chance of growing or changing. In the recovery world, this illusion is called "denial," the unwillingness to acknowledge our problem; in Buddhism it's called "wrong view," a distorted understanding of reality and ourselves. And so, the starting point for these twin paths is revealing ourselves—to ourselves and to others. We must look deeply and honestly at our thinking and our actions and admit our failings and our suffering. Until we take this first, often painful, step, we have no chance at recovery or happiness. Once we make these admissions, though, we discover that this self-revealing is actually the most freeing thing we can do.

In the section of each chapter called "What's This Step About?" I'll explain how I think each step fits into the archetypal path.

The Way of Mindfulness and Recovery

What is mindfulness? As this practice and Buddhist teachings have attracted more and more attention, the simple definitions once offered have been challenged by Buddhist scholars and dharma teachers, creating a bit of confusion about something that seems quite simple: the application of our attention to our mental and physical experience, moment by moment. I'm not qualified to enter into an academic debate on the topic, so I will give you my sense of the meaning of the word, and then encourage you to explore other sources if you'd like to understand more.

Mindfulness starts with being present, being aware of what we are experiencing through our five physical senses and what's happening in our mind. Our natural tendency is to get caught up worrying about or planning the future or remembering the past. The first thing we try to do with mindfulness is notice these tendencies and start to train ourselves to bring our attention back to what is happening right now. This alone is a huge task because of our deep conditioning. Planning the future based on our experiences in the past is a survival strategy developed eons ago by our ancestors. Our capacity to do this is what sets us apart from other living things, and so our instincts resist any effort to act otherwise. Nonetheless, these habits take us away from a direct experience of life and obscure a whole range of truths, from the psychological conditioning that drives our behavior to the elemental realities that Buddhists call "the Dharma," Truth or Natural Law.

With mindfulness we not only observe what's happening in the body and mind, but how we react to things, how a sound triggers a thought and a thought triggers an emotion and an emotion triggers a physical response. We begin to see the bigger picture, the process by which we construct our understanding of our world and who we are. This deconstruction of our experience is vitally important for addicts in or trying to get into recovery because it allows them to see how their addiction works and that there is a way out, that it's not inevitable or unstoppable. The process by which we become addicted is a mind/body process that can be reversed, and awareness is the first stepping-stone in that process. That's why Step One of the 12 Steps starts with the words "We admitted," because that admission is the bringing into our awareness the truth of our condition. Until we are aware of our condition, until we come out of denial, no recovery is possible. Step One is, essentially, an act of mindfulness, a clear seeing.

One of the things that's always struck me as unique about the Buddhist teachings is that the Buddha started out by talking about the difficulties in life, the suffering. This doesn't seem like the best marketing technique. If you want to sell a product, you shouldn't start out by being such a downer. And maybe that's one reason Buddhism seems to take hold slowly in a culture: it doesn't start out by promising paradise.

The practice of mindfulness then has a role in building from this recognition of suffering. The Buddha asks us to sit down (literally) and start to watch our experience unfold. If you sit still for a little while what you'll discover is that your mind is restless and filled with plans and memories that are agitating; your body doesn't want to sit still and often will begin to hurt or at least get itchy or tense; you start to fall asleep when you're trying to pay attention to the breath; sitting still becomes boring and tedious, not to mention frustrating as you try to follow the meditation instructions but fail repeatedly.

So, the first effect of mindfulness is to see the truth of the first Noble Truth—the Buddha was right, it's hard to be a human being. If we keep watching carefully, tracking the process moment-by-moment as we notice the mind wandering and gently come back to the breath, we see that when we let go of our obsessive thinking, we get moments of relief. Thus, we see the truth of the second and third Noble Truths: our discomfort is caused by our clinging and ends when we stop clinging. We also see, as Step One says, that we are powerless, in this case over the arising of thoughts, feelings, and sense experiences—not that we can't do anything about them, but that, just as with our addiction, they are going to keep coming up and if we are not going to suffer as they arise, we are going to have to change our relationship to them.

When an addict sees this meditative process clearly—and usually it helps if a teacher or guide clarifies what's happening—the logic of letting go becomes indisputable. We see in microcosm the process of addiction and recovery.

I know a couple of people who say that seeing this was enough for them to get clean and sober. They didn't have to go to rehab or AA or any other recovery program; all they needed was to see their addiction with mindfulness, and they were able to quit. But this is the rare exception. Before I got sober I seemed to be engaged in a pretty serious mindfulness meditation practice, even going on extended silent retreats, but still didn't make the connection between the microcosm of moment-to-moment letting go and the habitual patterns of drinking and using that persisted between retreats. The power of addiction and denial was just too great for my mindfulness practice alone to penetrate. There simply wasn't the willingness to go that far, and there wasn't the clarity to understand the problem and the potential that sobriety might bring.

Nonetheless, today I regularly teach mindfulness in treatment centers and to newcomers who attend my workshops and retreats. And I find that, if people are willing to learn and are engaged in trying to deal with their addiction, the mindfulness practices are a powerful support to the process of recovery. I think it helps that I guide them to understand what they are experiencing. Sometimes the non-verbal meditation experience is difficult to interpret at first, and this is one of the main jobs of the meditation teacher, to illuminate what is already happening, to understand the felt experience.

When I'm introducing mindfulness at a treatment center, I feel the need to explain why we're doing it. After all, when someone forks out money for rehab, it's not with the desire to learn to meditate. They might wonder, "What does this have to do with recovery?" I tell them that mindfulness meditation has two key values for the recovering addict: one, it helps them to de-stress. Recovery is stressful, in the beginning especially, and having a method by which you can, on a daily basis, get some quiet, calm, and peace, is invaluable. Two, mindfulness practice helps us to become aware of our mental habits so we can start to catch thoughts like, "I need to have a drink," or "What's the point of this, I might as well get loaded." Getting in the habit of watching and questioning our own thoughts is vital to maintaining recovery because the addict's habitual thoughts are so often self-destructive, or just simply destructive.

Mindfulness isn't magic or religious. Developing and applying mindfulness takes determination and effort. Nonetheless, it can have a powerful, liberating effect on our lives. All change starts with awareness, and when we cultivate mindfulness our awareness deepens far beyond our common way of experiencing life.

Mindfulness Meditation

A great deal has been written and said about mindfulness in recent years. This ancient spiritual tool has become trendy. And like all trends, people try to simplify it and package it in appealing and marketable ways. It's great that mindfulness has become popular, but vital, if we are going to engage in this path that we understand its full implications. While the basic idea of mindfulness can be fairly easy to grasp, integrating it into our lives, and learning to use it in meditation is a lifetime's practice.

I was first introduced to the concept of mindfulness in the spring of 1980. I'd already been practicing another form of meditation for two years and was interested in spirituality, even though I hadn't even begun to address my addiction. So, while I had a sincere desire to change, I was really in the early stages. At that point in my life I'd been making my living as a club musician for almost ten years, but had recently taken a day job, working in a health food store in Santa Monica, California. The produce manager had just gone on a meditation retreat with Joseph Goldstein and every time we had a break he and I and a few others would slip out the side door to hear him rave—if not *rant*—about what an amazing experience it had been sitting and walking silently for ten days in the desert.

Under all my spiritual longing was essentially a desire not to feel the pain in my life, the depression, anxiety, and craving that seemed to follow me around. This was, of course, the same desire that drove my drinking and using. So, when I heard about the meditation retreat, a lot of what I was interested in was the magical stuff—how *high* you could get. But as I began to study more, and when I got a hold of Joseph's book *The Experience of Insight*, what gave me real hope and trust in what he was teaching was how much sense it all made. Sure, there were mystical Zen stories and poems of enlightenment, but what ran through all of it was a practical, logical, and sensible understanding and approach to life. And the most basic element of that approach was the practice of mindfulness that simply said, "You need to be present, to pay attention to what's happening right now, if you want to grow and change." What could be more sensible? This wasn't about transcendence or faith, not God or even enlightenment, but rather about a simple tool for awakening in the present moment.

In Joseph's most recent book, simply called *Mindfulness*, he says that trying to briefly define mindfulness is like trying to briefly define "art" or "love." While that's probably true, I feel that I have to give you *something* to start with. So, here goes: Mindfulness is a focused, non-judgmental awareness of what is happening in the here and now. It is a level of present-moment awareness that takes us deeper than our common daily perception. It helps us to see our reactivity, our habitual thoughts and emotional patterns, to engage in our sense life more intimately, and to let go of the stresses of our daily lives.

Mindfulness can be practiced in any waking moment, in any posture, and potentially, in any situation. However, setting aside time to formally practice mindfulness in meditation is essential to developing any kind of broader mindfulness. Mindfulness meditation gives us the immediate benefit of calm and concentration that arises when we intentionally focus our attention, and it gives the ongoing benefit of strengthening our ability to *be* mindful and our understanding of the subtleties of mindfulness. Regularly practicing mindfulness meditation greatly increases the likelihood that at any given moment, we will *remember* to be mindful, which may be the most difficult aspect of the practice.

Mindfulness isn't about fixing ourselves, but, initially at least, about accepting who we are. It helps us to see into our own minds and the ways that we undermine ourselves and gives us the opportunity to make new choices based on our own wisdom.

My early experiences of mindfulness exposed me to the many ways I was missing my life. Mindful eating intensified my pleasure in tasting even the simplest foods; mindful walking connected me with my own body, how I held myself, and the tension that I often allowed to sit in my body; mindfulness of thoughts showed me how much of the time I spent planning, dreaming, fantasizing about how the future was going to be better than this moment. Soon I learned that I wasn't unique in any of this.

Most people spend their waking hours thinking about the future or the past. We worry and plan and fantasize; we remember, regret, and indulge in nostalgia. We calculate, analyze, and criticize. Mindfulness brings our attention into the present, into direct experience of what is, instead of staying lost in our thoughts. Mindfulness is getting at a simpler way of being alive, something more essential.

Mindfulness isn't just concentrating on something. That's a part of meditation, but mindfulness means that we are *aware of what we are aware of.* This can sound strange, and really, it can only be understood experientially. Mindfulness is a natural capacity in the human mind, and when we come to understand what it is and how to access it, it doesn't seem strange at all. In fact, when we begin to experience life in this way, the more common way of living can begin to look kind of strange instead.

Meditation itself is a great tool in the recovery process. Certainly the early stages of recovery are stressful and having a way to bring more calm and relaxation into our lives is very helpful. But even for the person with long-term recovery, having a practice that helps manage stress is vital. Many addicts tend to take on stress easily or react poorly to life's challenges. Having a way to work with these tendencies enhances the quality of life and reduces the likelihood of relapse. That's why Step Eleven, which suggests we meditate, is so vital to any ongoing 12-Step program.

Mindfulness meditation offers even more than "stress reduction," though. For one, it gives us insight into our own minds, helping us to see the habitual thought patterns and emotional reactions that are at the root of our addiction. As we start to understand ourselves more clearly, we become less the victim of those destructive qualities, more able to let go of negative and distorted views of ourselves and of the world. In 12-Step parlance, we can call this a kind of meditative inventory, a check on ourselves and our perception of reality.

Further, mindfulness meditation can connect us to a feeling of something greater, a sense of meaning and purpose in our lives. If we are willing to do the regular work of meditation, we begin to have a spiritual experience that gives us a feeling of our own wholeness as well as a sense of the preciousness of life and the world around us. This deeper connection is one of the most powerful effects of meditation. Many people in recovery hunger for this connection and depend on their meditation practice to instill their lives with meaning.

While all of this is possible with mindfulness meditation, the practice itself works with the most basic elements of our human experience, just those things that are happening to us moment-to-moment in our body and mind. Rather than aiming for lofty experiences, mindfulness practice directs us to these simple elements of life, letting their meaning and beauty reveal themselves over time.

I'm going to take you through the different ways that we can be mindful. We start by applying these forms of attention in our formal meditation practice, but ultimately want to bring this kind of attention to all our activities. For each of these approaches to mindfulness I'll offer an introductory meditation.

* * *

Paying attention to the body means being aware of sense experiences, sounds, sensations, sights, tastes, smells. Mindfulness meditation usually begins by focusing on the sensations of breath—

an aspect of body awareness. As we become more attuned to our sense experience, it helps us let go of stress and take care of ourselves. We become more sensitive to what we take into the body and what we do with it. This all trends toward greater health and well-being.

My guided meditations will help you understand how to work with awareness of the body. Just paying attention to the breath can have a calming effect. Returning over and over to the breath when the mind wanders helps to stabilize and concentrate the mind as well as bringing a sense of calm and relaxation to the body.

The breath is usually a fairly neutral sensation, but that's not true of every feeling in the body. As we sit still, many feelings may appear, an itch, some muscle tightness, pain in the back or knees. Whatever happens in the body, we try to open to that as part of our mindfulness practice. There's the tendency to want to fix any unpleasant sensation, but that tendency will break your concentration, and is essentially an expression of the same aversion that leads to addiction. I'll explain this further in the section on the Five Hindrances, but simply put, what causes addiction in the first place is our tendency to want all pleasure and no pain. When we are sitting in meditation, if discomfort comes up, rather than pushing it away or trying to avoid it, we open to it, bringing an accepting and non-reactive attitude that becomes a kind of microcosm of the recovery process itself, which inevitably involves physical and emotional discomfort. If we are going to maintain our recovery, we are going to have to learn to live with certain degrees of discomfort, at least occasionally. So, our meditation practice becomes a training ground for learning how to do this.

To learn more about working with pain in meditation, or if you are dealing with more severe or chronic pain, please look at the section on pain in Step Seven.

Just a word about some other meditation techniques that involve sense awareness. The practice called "sweeping," which you'll find in the guided meditations, takes us through the whole body, bit by bit, exploring each sensation we encounter. This powerful practice can deepen concentration as well as bring a strong sense of the impermanence of our moment-to-moment experience. Using this practice brings us into a much deeper awareness of our life as embodied beings. It also connects well with a yoga, Qi Gong, or other movement practice, and, in fact, will support any workout routine.

The other sense practice that is very helpful is using sound as a central focus. Listening creates a shift from the more narrow awareness with breath or sensations into a more open, spaciousness. I recommend that you work with the sound meditation as well and discover for yourself how this feels. If you find yourself struggling with trying to cling to the breath or with a sense of tension or anxiety, it can be very helpful to shift perspective to this more spacious awareness. By listening to sounds, we get a sense of our mind as going beyond the limits of the body, as sounds come from all over, from nearby and far away. Sound has a lightness that can be uplifting. While people who are learning meditation often think that any noise is a distraction, this approach welcomes all the ambient sound into our awareness. In this way, we use what might seem to be an annoyance as the foundation for an easeful attention.

As you'll see in the Attitudes of Mindfulness section, all of these practices are founded in the qualities of patience and acceptance. Learning to move from the desire to control our experience into a relaxed and receptive mode of attention immediately reduces our struggles with mind and body.

Meditation: Introduction to Mindfulness - The Breath

Read through this section, and then close the book and follow the instructions. For this first mindfulness practice, don't worry too much about posture, just sit comfortably. Begin by closing your eyes and just feeling your body breathing. You'll notice that the chest and belly are rising and falling as you breathe, and that there is a gentle and subtle sensation at the nostrils as the air passes in and out. Pay attention to each of these places, belly, chest, and nostrils one by one, spending a few breaths at each point. Then settle your attention on one of these places. It doesn't matter which, just wherever you feel like it right now. Spend a few minutes becoming familiar with the feeling of the breath at this "anchor point." When your mind wanders and you realize you're not paying attention to the breath, just bring the attention back and start again.

Do this exercise for just few minutes. Don't push yourself, just try to get a feel for this basic approach. When you're ready, open your eyes.

* * *

Paying attention to mind means noticing our thoughts. This is very challenging and takes some practice. We're used to just accepting and believing everything we think, but mindfulness asks us to observe our thoughts, to question them, and to become aware of the habitual, conditioned ways we think so that we can discover whether our thoughts are true and whether they are useful. It's said that "all experience is preceded by mind," that is, our thoughts create our perception of reality. So, if we can become more aware of our thoughts, we can make wiser choices that will improve our lives.

Of course, for the addict this isn't just a theoretical issue. It's a life and death issue. We have to learn a whole new way of thinking about ourselves and about the world. We have to move from a controlling, cynical, and grasping attitude to one of accepting and dealing with "life on life's terms." This begins by just seeing the ways we think, and then choosing to let go and open to other viewpoints.

At the end of one meditation session at a daylong retreat I taught, one of the participants raised her hand and said, "I didn't realize how much time I spend thinking about work." This was a simple, but vital, realization. It was a Saturday; she wasn't at work; she was meditating; she didn't need to be thinking about work. While thinking about work isn't the worst thing, why spend your meditation doing it? If you begin to study your own thoughts, you will find many unproductive streams of thought. And you'll discover that just by noticing what you are thinking, oftentimes you'll be able to let go right in that moment. Of course, the thoughts might come back, but over time you'll undermine their power by letting them go repeatedly.

The point of mindfulness meditation isn't to stop thinking. Sometimes your thoughts may slow down or become quieter, but even if they don't, just seeing them is incredibly useful. If you are in risk of relapse, noticing thoughts about using can be a vital alarm to tell you that you need to take some action to strengthen your recovery; if you tend towards depression, mindfulness can help to weaken the negative thought patterns that spiral into trouble; if you get swept up in anxiety, seeing the irrationality of your fears can defuse those triggers; when you struggle in a relationship, seeing all the underlying thoughts of blame or resentment can help you to break out of those destructive views and get a more balanced understanding of what's going on.

While mindfulness of the body is perhaps the most effective calming and concentrating aspect of mindfulness meditation, mindfulness of thoughts is the most revealing and psychologically insightful.

Meditation: Introduction to Mindfulness - Thoughts

Read through this section, and then close the book and follow the instructions. Begin by closing your eyes and practicing mindful breathing. As soon as you notice that you are thinking instead of paying attention to your breath, open your eyes. Ask yourself, "What was I just thinking?" Review what the thought was; how long were you caught in the thought? What kind of thought was it? A plan? A memory? A worry? Did it have a quality of desire or aversion?

Close your eyes again, and repeat the exercise.

Do this three times.

Now you are beginning to see your own thoughts.

* * *

Paying attention to emotions means engaging our emotions on the visceral level. This is directly connected to body mindfulness. Instead of thinking about our feelings or reacting to them in some negative way, we simply feel. What does anger feel like? What does fear or sadness or joy feel like? So much of the time we just get caught up in our emotions, acting unconsciously on feelings. When we bring awareness to emotions, again we gain more control of our lives. Instead of acting impulsively, we learn to just feel our emotions and reflect on them. As we see them clearly, we are able to make more wise choices that also improve our lives.

For the addict, getting a handle on our feelings may the most important element of mindfulness practice in preventing relapse. Whether in our first thirty days or ten years down the line, feelings happen; anger arises; grief engulfs us; anxiety sweeps over us; depression drowns us. Even if we don't drink or use over these feelings, they can drain all the happiness from our lives. Mindfulness practice with its focus on the present moment, on the body, and on the impermanence of all experience gives us a unique way of relating to and holding emotions. When we remind ourselves that this is just a feeling, it helps us to not be overwhelmed; when we feel the emotion in the body, it grounds us and calms us; when we remember that this isn't going to last forever, it gives us some relief from the sense of oppression that emotions can bring. All of this is part of the practice of mindfulness of emotions that we'll explore.

Meditation: Introduction to Mindfulness - Emotions

Read through this section, and then close the book and follow the instructions. Begin by closing your eyes and taking several mindful breaths. Then, put your attention into your torso, the chest and belly. Ask yourself, "What mood or emotion am I feeling right now?" See if there is a word that captures your mood. It's okay if the mood is undefinable, as long as you can *feel* it. Or the mood or emotion might be multifaceted, not just one thing. That's fine. The important thing is to *sense* the mood or emotion.

Now, breathe into this part of the body and relax. Let the mood be there without trying to change it. Notice if just by watching it the mood does change, growing stronger, weaker, or turning into something else.

Breathe again and open your eyes.

Meditation: Body Scan

This is a simplified version of a classic Vipassana meditation sometimes called "sweeping." You can find more extensive versions of this in Jon Kabat-Zinn's books and in Ayya Khema's *When the Iron Eagle Flies*. (She calls it "Part by Part".) I often use this as an introduction to a longer guided meditation to help people get relaxed and into their bodies.

Read through this section, and then close the book and follow the instructions. Begin by closing your eyes and taking several mindful breaths. As you go through the parts of the body to relax, feel any sensations in that part of the body.

Begin by bringing your attention to the muscles in the face. Relax your jaw. Just let the jaw be slack, while keeping the mouth closed. Relax the small muscles around the eyes. Relax the forehead.

Now move the attention down, relaxing the neck and shoulders, making sure the shoulders aren't hunched. Relax the arms and hands. Feel the sensations in the hands.

Now bring the attention to the chest and belly and soften and open that part of the body, letting the breath move deeply into the belly.

Relax the large muscles in the back. As you breathe, feel the back expand and contract, and on an out-breath, release any tension.

Relax through the pelvis and hips. Relax the legs and feet, feeling the sensations in the feet.

Now take a moment to see if you can feel the whole body at once, as a single object. Then, notice that within this single object, there are many different sensations happening at once. For a moment, see if you can hold these two perspectives at once, the single body and the myriad sensations.

Exercise: Full Mindfulness Meditation

This section combines and amplifies the previous sections into a complete meditation. This guided meditation should take at least 20 minutes. You can try recording it, reading slowly, and then listening to the instructions, or you can study it and try to remember it as you practice. For a group, one member might read the instructions aloud while the rest follow along. If you are reading or recording this, read slowly, allowing the listeners time to absorb and follow the instructions. Generally, it is easier to learn meditation from a live instructor, but if there's no available teacher, you can use this guidance or some other resource.

Posture

The way we sit has a direct effect on the way we feel, particularly on our energetic state. In meditation, the key component of posture is a straight back. We can sit on a chair or on a cushion on the floor with the legs crossed; either way is fine. If you are sitting on a chair, place both feet flat on the floor. If you are sitting on a cushion, use one of the traditional yoga lotus poses (half-lotus, full-lotus, etc.). Sitting on a cushion may make you feel more "Buddhist," but it's also more challenging. Since sitting still is more important than how you look, if you can't maintain a lotus posture for at least twenty minutes without moving, I suggest you use a chair. Of course, if your body is relatively healthy and flexible, a regular yoga practice will help you develop the capacity to sit on a cushion.

Gently close your eyes, or if you're not comfortable sitting with your eyes closed, simply lower your gaze. Try to align the head, neck, and body so that you have created a balanced posture, not tipping forward, back, or to the side.

With your posture, try to create a balance between being relaxed and comfortable, and staying alert and awake. If you get into a rigid posture, you just create stress and pain; but if you slump and loll, you'll tend to get sleepy and dull. See if you can find that place of balance.

Body scan/relaxation

Now we'll do some conscious relaxation in order to settle in. As we go through the parts of the body to relax, feel any sensations in that part of the body.

Begin by bringing your attention to the muscles in the face. Relax your jaw. Just let the jaw be slack, while keeping the mouth closed. Relax the small muscles around the eyes. Relax the forehead.

Now move the attention down, relaxing the neck and shoulders, making sure the shoulders aren't hunched. Relax the arms and hands. Feel the sensations in the hands.

Now bring the attention to the chest and belly and soften and open that part of the body, letting the breath move deeply into the belly.

Relax the large muscles in the back. As you breathe, feel the back expand and contract, and on an out-breath, release any tension.

Relax through the pelvis and hips. Relax the legs and feet, feeling the sensations in the feet.

Now take a moment to see if you can feel the whole body at once, as a single object. Then, notice that within this single object, there are many different sensations happening at once. For a moment, see if you can hold these two perspectives at once, the single body and the myriad sensations.

Breath

Now we'll begin to work with the breath. Feel the whole breath as it moves through the body, the air entering and leaving the nostrils, the movement of the chest and belly. After feeling a few breaths like this, see where it's easiest for you to feel and follow the breath, the nostrils, the chest, or the belly. Now make that single point the center of your meditation.

If you are following the breath at the nostrils, notice the sensations of the air coming in and the sensations of the air going out. If you are following the breath in the chest or belly, notice the sensations of the movement of the body. There's nothing special you're trying to feel, just whatever you can perceive. We're simply trying to train the attention to become more subtle and stable. Don't try to breathe in any particular way, just allow the body to breathe as it will, and try to be aware of how that feels.

Now, notice the difference between the sensation of breathing in and the sensation of breathing out. Two distinct experiences. We want to start to examine the details of the breath.

If it's helpful you can make a soft mental note to help guide and hold the attention. If you're following the breath at the nostrils, you can note, "In, out" as you breathe in and out; if you're following the breath at the chest or belly, you can note, "Rising, falling," or "Up, down." The words should be very soft, in the background of the mind, while awareness of the actual sensations is in the foreground.

Letting go of thoughts

It's quite natural that we drift into thinking as we try to stay with the breath. How we work with thoughts is an important part of practice. When you realize that your attention has wandered into thinking, just acknowledge that thinking is happening, and gently come back to the sensations of breath. Try not to add a judgment or commentary. You haven't made a mistake or blown it. In fact, the moment of realizing you're thinking is a moment of mindfulness, of waking up.

Once you've let go of the thought, it's as though you were beginning the meditation again. It's often helpful to take a deeper, relaxing breath then, letting go of any tension that arose when you were lost in thought, then settling back into the focus on breathing.

Sometimes when you notice that you are thinking, the thought will just dissolve and it will be easy to come back to the breath. Other times there will seem to be a steady stream of thoughts that, even when acknowledged, continue on. If you find this happening, see if you can let those thoughts move into the background of your experience, while keeping sensations of breath in the foreground. Those thoughts can be like a CNN scroll on the bottom of your TV screen, or like the sound of traffic in the background. Don't be bothered by them. If they aren't capturing your attention, if you aren't getting lost in them, you can just leave them alone and keep following the breath.

Deepening awareness of breath

If you can, start to become aware of more and more subtle sensations in the breath. Each breath is unique. See if you can feel that uniqueness. The breath can be broken down into distinct components: the beginning of the breath; the inflow; the end of the inflow; the beginning of the out breath; the outflow; the end of the out breath. Sometimes there's a space between breaths. If that happens, just keep the attention at that point in the body where you are following the breath.

The breath can have many different textures and tones: rough, smooth; subtle, distinct; warm, cool; long, short. Sometimes the breath will seem to disappear all together. Relax and try to feel whatever is arising.

Developing a Practice

Many people take a meditation class and then have a hard time developing the discipline to maintain a regular practice. There are some internal qualities that help, and some external elements.

We need to be committed to our practice. Why are you practicing? Have you seen the value of it in your life or in the life of others? Have you been inspired by something you've read or someone you've studied with? Has a friend or relative gotten something out of it? Or do you just intuitively sense that this is what you need in your life? Think about what it is that interests and inspires you about meditation; perhaps write some of these things down. Absorb deeply this longing; take it in. Let it become a part of you so that there's no doubt, no ambivalence about practice. This deep personal sense of the value and importance of practice can be a resource for you, a touchstone.

This commitment is called "intention," and it needs to be understood, not as something we have to do or we've failed, but as a basic guideline for our lives. It's not helpful to set goals of perfection. Rather, whenever we notice that our commitment is slackening, we try to reinvigorate ourselves. Just as in the meditation, when the mind wanders we come back to the breath, when our larger life wanders, we come back to meditating. Set a goal, perhaps to meditate 6 days a week. If you come up short, don't beat yourself up. This is about awareness: just notice if you didn't make it this week, and recommit yourself to next week. Notice, too, if you are making meditation into a job, another unpleasant obligation, or if you are creating more pressure on yourself to live up to some standard of perfection.

We have to be careful not to try too hard and not to slack off. We look for a balance, a middle route between striving perfectionism and lazy apathy. If you are like most people, at times you'll fall into one or the other, or even both of these. That's natural; that's human. If you get angry with yourself about it, you're just creating more problems. Can you accept your "failure" and start again?

Tips for Practice

1. Set up a place in your home devoted to meditation. This can just be a corner of a room, or a small extra space or alcove. Put your

chair or meditation cushion in the corner, and perhaps a small table with some special objects. Having a space devoted to meditation acts as a reminder to practice, and reinforces the practice when you sit there.

2. Schedule meditation into your day. Before you go to bed at night, decide when you are going to meditate the next day. You might have to get up earlier or leave some gaps in your schedule. You can meditate on a break or at lunchtime at work; you can meditate before dinner; you can even meditate before bed, though that's not ideal.

3. Commit to meditate every day, even if it's only for 1 minute. This commitment helps you sustain your practice. It reinforces the idea that consistency is the most important thing, not perfection.

4. Find a meditation group and/or teacher. Nothing reinforces practice like regularly joining others to meditate. Just as with recovery, it's hard to do it alone. Take advantage of the support that's out there.

Attitudes of Mindfulness

There are certain attitudes that will help you with your mindfulness practice. These attitudes all work together, supporting and informing each other.

Non-Judging

The tendency of the mind is to be constantly assessing our experience, ourselves, and others. In meditation this often appears either as a judgment of our own practice or of what is happening as we practice. We'll automatically put a label of "good" or "bad" on ourselves and everything that happens.

So, if we find that we have a hard time quieting the mind, that it seems as if the whole meditation period is spent thinking and not being aware of the breath, we might fall into thinking, "I'm no good at this," or "I'm not doing this right." It's important that we catch this kind of thinking and remember to categorize it as thinking. We try to take the stance of an impartial observer. That means that a mindful response to the thought, "This is boring," is noticing that we are making a judgment. Sooner or later, as you start to notice judging, you may find yourself thinking, "I shouldn't be judging so much," and that is just more judging—judging the judgments. These are very powerful habits of mind. They aren't going to stop just because we decide they should or because we try to be aware of the breath. However, just learning to notice judgments objectively will have the natural effect of reducing our attachment and belief in our judging thoughts. This lets us begin to take a more objective view of our experience.

Patience

The ability to be mindful develops over time. How much time, there's no saying. It's different for each person. When we first sit down to meditate we might have some hope that something is going to happen, and if it doesn't, we might get impatient. If we can just relax and trust in the process, it will unfold and develop. If we are trying to rush the process or get impatient, we actually undermine the natural quieting that the mind inclines to.

Again, the attitude of observing our experience, rather than trying to control it, allows us to just sit with whatever is appearing, whether it's pleasant, unpleasant, or neutral. As we develop this quality of patience, we become less reactive and more balanced in our response to experiences. We don't feel the same urgency to fix or change things that we don't like. This in turn increases our inner peace and leads to more patience, more willingness to be with things just as they are.

Acceptance

When we come to meditation it's often with the hope of accomplishing something, whether we want more peace in our lives, to let go of stress, to feel more connected, more wise, or to develop an open-heart. But we can't make these things happen. If we are always trying to change the way we feel, then we'll never find peace or connection. The attitude of mindfulness is, "What is happening right now? Can I just be with this without trying to change it?" This attitude of open acceptance points us back to the present moment and to letting go of goals, judgments, and striving.

It's very common in meditation to fall into traps, though. Even though in principle we agree with the idea of being accepting, something might happen that doesn't seem right. Maybe someone comes in the room and slams a door. We think, "Don't they know I'm meditating? Why don't they quiet down." A mindful, accepting attitude might be more like, "That was an unpleasant sound," and then noticing the irritation and the desire for things to be quiet.

Acceptance says, "Things are as they are. If you fight that, you just cause yourself more stress and discomfort; if you can accept things as they are, many of your petty irritations will just fall away."

Be careful, though, because acceptance isn't the answer to every situation. Some things shouldn't be accepted, and as the Serenity Prayer says, we need to learn to discern the difference between what should be accepted and what we should work to change. Mindfulness isn't about passively accepting everything, but rather getting a more accurate understanding of what's happening. Nonetheless, learning to accept things as they are is an important starting point because of the tendency to try to control everything.

Curiosity

When it comes down to it, mindfulness is an exploration of life. We are looking closely at things that we usually take for granted, our body sensations, sounds, thoughts, and emotions. If we bring an attitude of interest, of curiosity, we discover that many of these mundane experiences hold within themselves rich moments to discover. This is, after all, what life is really made up of, these moment- to-moment experiences. Mindfulness helps us to make the most of life.

When we bring curiosity to each moment of meditation and each moment of life, things get much more interesting. One formula says, "Boredom is the lack of attention," which implies that if you just pay attention—*to whatever is happening*—that it will be interesting. When we first start to meditate, we immediately realize that there is a world of experience that we've been missing out on. That can serve as motivation for looking more closely. If just paying attention to my breath reveals so much, what will I discover if I start to pay attention more fully to the rest of my life?

Non-Identification

We tend to take things personally. "My thoughts, my breath, my feelings." Mindfulness encourages us to take another view: just thoughts, breath, and feelings—not mine, not me. This radical shift in perspective helps us to maintain an objective viewpoint. Every time we take things personally, we're adding a layer to our experience that tends to complicate matters. If I think a thought is "mine," then I tend to judge it more; I think that I have to do something about it; I think that I am either "good" or "bad" based on whether it's a good or bad thought.

Notice that what I've just described is several extra layers of thinking, whereas, if I just see the thought as words or images in the mind, not necessarily "mine," then I don't have to do anything about the thought, just see it and accept it.

If I identify thoughts as mine, I also tend to react emotionally. I've given the thought meaning, and that meaning triggers feelings in me. If I see the thought objectively, I don't tend to react in these ways.

Of course, we are deeply conditioned to identify with our thoughts and feelings—as well as our physical sensations. We can't just turn conditioning like this off. But we can start to notice how we identify. Bringing that investigative curiosity to our experience helps us to begin to break the habit of conditioned response.

Letting Go

Letting go is the antidote to the habitual way of clinging to thoughts and feelings. The simple practice of returning to the breath when you notice that you are thinking shows the power of letting go. Oftentimes we'll have a sense of relief and release when we come back to the breath. Our habitual way of being is to pursue streams of thought, to follow them wherever they go, letting them control and lock up our minds. When we start to meditate we see how this way of handling thoughts actually causes pain, or at least a sense of unease, stress, or restlessness. The meditation practice shows us the value of the simple act of dropping thoughts. This experience can inform our lives in important ways.

When we start to examine our experience with curiosity and non-identification, we can begin to be more objective about what works and what doesn't in our life, what brings more happiness and what brings more unhappiness. We soon discover that things that might have seemed so important, like our judgments about people, are really not worth the stress they cause. Instead of being so attached to being right, we might realize that being happy is more worthwhile.

This internal experience can also be mirrored in our external experience. Sometimes we see that things we own or activities we do are more of a burden than a blessing. The spirit of letting go is to examine our lives, inside and out, and see what is really working for us and what is not. Then we begin to make decisions based on these insights. It doesn't mean that we have to make any radical changes in our lives, just that we start to question our habitual ways of being, and start making choices based on mindful observation rather than the coercive effects of internal conditioning or social pressure. Letting go is actually the most immediate way to happiness.

FAQs

Q: It seems like you're saying I shouldn't have any opinions on things. Is mindfulness just becoming passive and not caring about anything?

A: With mindfulness, we're not trying to stop having opinions. That's probably not possible, anyway. We just want to become more aware where our opinions are coming from. They are thoughts in the mind.

They may have some logical basis, or they might just be conditioned responses. Mindfulness helps us to see that our opinions aren't necessarily true. And it also helps us to see how when we are judgmental or closed-minded we are limiting ourselves and often creating suffering for ourselves, and maybe others, too.

Q: I'm an impatient person. You say I'll get more patience if I sit still, but how am I supposed to sit still if I'm impatient?

A: It is a kind of Catch-22. One way to handle this is to start slowly. Just do 5 minutes of meditation to start with, or even 1 minute. Each time you meditate, try to stretch it a little more: "Okay, I made it 5 minutes, let's see if I can do 6 or 7 next time." You might find that once you get started it's not as hard as you think.

Q: It seems like mindfulness is all about being passive. You say "accept things," but there are some things I don't think I should accept, like a violent criminal or an abusive boss. Am I just supposed to let people walk all over me?

A: Acceptance is only one part of mindfulness. It's a starting point that we accept, "this is how things are." But then, we can decide whether we need to do something to change things. The difference is that with mindfulness we have a choice, we are conscious and careful. If we aren't mindful, then we just react impulsively out of our conditioned habits. That's just running on automatic pilot, acting unconsciously from our base instincts. If we look at a situation mindfully, we can make the decision whether there is something we want to do about the situation and consider if that's a wise decision. Mindfulness is helping us to be more conscious and wise.

Q: It seems like if I'm going to be mindful I have to do everything really slowly and carefully. When I meditate I'm just sitting still

and feeling my breath. But how am I supposed to do my work or hang out with my friends or family and do everything so slowly and mindfully?

A: When we meditate or do mindfulness exercises, we do slow down so that we can get the feel of mindfulness and so that we can train ourselves to pay attention more. But we can be mindful at any speed. Try it next time you're doing the dishes or sweeping the floor. All you have to do is direct your mind to be aware of what you're doing, and you can be mindful. Of course, when you're meditating you can be more closely mindful, but once you understand what mindfulness is you can apply it to any activity at any speed.

Q: If my thoughts aren't me or mine, what is? Isn't that what I am, my thoughts?

A: This is a classic philosophical question. Mindfulness doesn't tell us what to believe. It only gives us tools for exploring these questions. Keep looking and asking yourself "Who am I?" Many people have had profound insights by contemplating this fundamental question.

Q: If I'm supposed to let go of everything, won't I wind up homeless and with no family? That doesn't sound so great.

A: We certainly don't have to give up our basic comforts to get the benefits of mindfulness. The larger point is to see how clinging to things causes us problems and pain. Then we can decide if there's something we need to let go of. Material things are probably the least of things that we cling to. It might be worth noting, though, that many of the greatest spiritual teachers renounced material possessions. But it's more important to let go of your anger, judgment and fear than it is to let go of your car or your computer.

PART ONE: SURRENDER

Steps One, Two, and Three are the surrender Steps. They are the time when we relinquish past behaviors, viewpoints, and attachments. Not only do we stop acting on our addiction, but we start looking for an entirely new orientation in our lives, seeking not just pleasure and personal gratification, but to do what's right. We come to understand that in the longer, more mature, recovered view, we must sometimes take actions that don't feel comfortable right now but will lead to more beneficial results than the impulsive behaviors we've been caught up in.

For the Newcomer

Much of this book can be used at any stage of recovery, but I wanted to particularly address the issues of those who are at the beginning of this process. I offer these thoughts if you are either not sure that you have an addiction problem or are just getting started with your recovery. I'm not suggesting that these teachings will be enough to establish your recovery without a 12 Step program, treatment center, or some other work. Nonetheless, I hope this section will help in your early recovery process.

Was I Really That Bad? Powerless Over Your Addiction

If we are going to establish ourselves in recovery, we are going to have to fully accept the truth that we can no longer do what we've been doing, that our addictive behaviors, whether substance-(drugs, alcohol, food), process-(relationships), or activity-(sex, gambling, work) oriented don't work. In 12 Step work we call this "admitting our powerlessness." If you have trouble with the word "powerless" and feel that it somehow demeans you or implies weakness, or that you simply don't feel powerless, don't use that word. You might just say, "I can't always control my behavior," especially once you start the addictive activity. Another simple way of approaching the question of whether you need to quit or not is to ask, "Is this behavior helping me, and might things be better in my life if I quit."

I find a lot of people get stuck on the idea of "am I an alcoholic?" or "am I an addict?" And I don't think that's the important question. What I've come to see is, whether I could be clinically diagnosed as an addict or not, as long as I was drinking and using drugs I couldn't deal with the problems in my life. Perhaps my addiction wasn't my biggest problem, but as long as it was there, it was keeping me from dealing with (notice I don't say "solving") my other problems. Today, I still have problems, but I can deal with them. Life is full of problems, and drinking and using just makes it harder to deal with them—and often creates other problems.

Exercise: What It Was Like

This exercise can be done as a writing process, a sharing process, or a contemplative process. The main thing is to be honest. Totally honest.

When speakers tell their stories at 12 Step meetings, the classic format is to describe "what it was like, what happened, and what it's like now." This exercise covers just the first part of that formula.

Go through in detail every case where you acted on your addiction and the results weren't good. Start with your earliest memories, maybe getting caught drinking, getting sick, blacking out; perhaps you missed school, crashed a car, got arrested. What about violence? Emotional outbursts?

Did you waste money? Damage relationships? Waste professional opportunities?

How many times did you act like a jerk? Take foolish risks? Sleep with someone you didn't know or care about?

How did your addiction affect your emotional states, causing depression, anxiety, anger, apathy, mania, irritability, or any other moods?

You get the idea, and I'm sure you can come up with your own consequences. The important thing isn't to remember every single event, but to establish in your conscious mind the persistent nature of the destructive effects of your addiction. This is fundamental to destroying any vestige of denial, so that you never again can tell yourself, "It wasn't that bad." Sure, it might not have been "that bad" every time or all the time, but if you look at the whole scope of your addiction, the years it dragged on and all the ways it hurt you and others, it's bound to make an impression. That's the result we want from this exercise.

Writing all this down and sharing it with a sponsor or other trusted person is a great way to embed a basic truth in your mind: *It doesn't work!*

Exercise: Cost-Benefit Analysis

Often when I'm talking to someone who is struggling with whether they want or need to get clean and sober or not, the question comes up of how important to their happiness their drinking and using is. Of course, the classic "I love wine with dinner," is a standard worry. But what is perhaps more common, and what I experienced when faced with this decision, was the fear that all the fun would go out of my life if I stopped drinking and smoking pot. It was only when I got sober that I realized how little fun I'd actually been having for the past ten or fifteen years, and that even before that, the state of inebriation I'd so often achieved left me with a feeling of emptiness and lots of regrets. Finally, I discovered that in sobriety I was *more able to enjoy life*, that the clarity, health, and energy that came with being sober, along with the newfound sense of connection with others in 12-Step programs, enriched my life much further than the supposedly mood-lifting effects of beer and pot that I'd used on a daily basis to have "fun." In fact it stopped being fun a long time before, if it ever really was.

Here's the exercise: Make three columns on a sheet of paper. In the first column write down the benefits you get from your addictive behaviors, whether, emotional, social, or anything else. In the second column write the costs, social, emotional, professional, physical, economic, etc. Here you need to be what AA calls "rigorously honest." Maybe you don't have cirrhosis of the liver, but what about a cough from smoking cigarettes or pot? Hangovers? Fights with your partner? What could you have done with all the money you've spent? In the third column, write down potential benefits from dropping your addiction, again, social, physical, financial, etc.

If you don't see that you might benefit from dealing with your behavior, then maybe you don't want or need to read this book.

Powerlessness and Surrender

Many people, especially when trying to decide if they want to go to a 12 Step program, find themselves alienated by the word *powerless* in Step One. It seems to be disempowering—literally—and runs counter to our cultural belief in self-reliance and personal responsibility. The Big Book of Alcoholics Anonymous lists all the ways that the early members tried to control their drinking in a passage that becomes darkly humorous as it recites the contradictory and finally absurd lengths that they had gone to try to manage their problem: "Drinking beer only, limiting the number of drinks, never drinking alone, never drinking in the morning, drinking only at home, never having it in the house, . . . taking a trip, not taking a trip. . . " The emphasis here and in many other passages in the book is on the utter lack of control that the true alcoholic has once they take the first drink. But this book was written by and for what we might call "hopeless drunks," people who have tried over and over and failed to control their drinking, while their lives, their families, their jobs all went down the drain.

There are plenty of people today just like this, and I've met many of them. However, many of the people coming into 12-Step programs now aren't so hopeless. They fall more into the category of what Anne Fletcher, author of the book *Sober for Good*, calls "problem drinkers." And one of the distinctions of the problem drinker is that she may not binge every time she has a drink. Sometimes she might have a couple glasses of wine and be fine, but at other times, a binge may follow. The problem is, *she never knows what will happen.* If you can control your drinking some of the time, but at other times you lose control, can you claim that you are *ever* actually in control?

* * *

One of the arguments against powerlessness that people who have studied Buddhism put forward is that "Buddhism is about self-reliance. We're all responsible for our own enlightenment. If we just make Right Effort we can achieve enlightenment on our own," and presumably sobriety as well. This interpretation of Buddhism reflects a particularly Western, maybe American, bias. While the Buddha pointed to the importance of our own effort in achieving freedom, he never said that individuals were in control of everything. In fact, one of the things he emphasizes in his teachings is our *lack* of control over our bodies, our thoughts, and our feelings: in regards to these, he says, "This is not mine, this I am not, this is not my self." In the First Noble Truth he tells us that sickness, old age, and death are the inevitable results of being born. He says that everything we love is bound to change. If all of this is true, then can't we say that we are powerless over—that is we don't control—our bodies, thoughts, and feelings?

This doesn't mean that we don't have some influence over these things. In fact, one vital purpose of mindfulness practice is to change our relationship to our minds and bodies. And the purpose of powerlessness in the 12 Steps is to change our relationship to our addiction. Perhaps one way of turning Step One around is to say, "Alcohol (drugs, etc.) is very powerful, and that power overwhelms me." The same is true of our minds and bodies. Mindfulness practice is a tool for handling the power of these things. Our old ways of dealing with life—and addiction—don't work; battling with life, trying to control things is a futile task. The mindful response is to disengage from the battle and the effort to control, to move into a stance of observing, of feeling, of sensing. From that stance we begin to learn how to dance with all these energies, with the craving to drink, with our obsessive thoughts, with the pain in our bodies, with our depression, anxiety, anger, and despair. Mindfulness is neither suppressing nor indulging, it is a completely different way of relating to our experience, to our lives. It requires a subtle, observing intelligence, a surrender to what is and a willingness to see things differently.

Surrender is a spiritual principle similar to powerlessness. One neutral way of understanding surrender is to say that it expresses the recognition of the vast power of the universe and our place in it. While theistic religions interpret this by surrendering to God, in Buddhism we surrender, or take refuge in Buddha, Dharma, and Sangha. I'll explore the idea of refuge later in the book, but for now, we can say that Dharma means Truth, and when we surrender to that Truth we are expressing a wise humility. This is what the First Noble Truth is pointing to. Surrender to the Truth contains nothing of the failure or defeat implicit in the word, but rather a bowing to the power of what is: in Buddhist terms, the power of suffering and craving; in recovery terms, the power of addiction. To try to fight with this greater Truth reminds me of the title to the

Broadway show "Your Arms Too Short to Box with God." If you're an addict, your arms are definitely too short to box with your addiction.

When the Steps say we are powerless, they are setting us up to be "saved" by God, in some sense, and that is the next problem that the non-theist will find in the Steps. I'll address that issue in later Steps, but right now, what I want to say is that for many people in recovery, surrender to their inability to drink or use or act out their addiction was the most *freeing* experience of their lives. People often discover, rather than feeling a loss at quitting, that they feel a great relief as the burden of managing their addiction is lifted, the cloud of intoxication clears, and the chains of craving fall away. This same sense of freedom comes when we accept the Truth of Suffering, that we aren't responsible for making the world or our lives perfect, that the challenges and struggles of life are the natural result of the way things are.

Exercise: Powerless, not Helpless

The irony for many of us is that, while we didn't want to admit our powerlessness over alcohol and maybe a lot of other things, we might have been all too ready to abdicate responsibility for things we didn't want to deal with. **Here's the exercise**: Make a list of things that you *try* to control which are actually not under your control; then make a list of the things you *can control* but avoid dealing with.

Exercise: Control Yourself

One of the ways that many of us maintain denial about our addiction is that we appear to be controlling our behavior. I did this by counting drinks and being very aware of how much pot I was smoking—everyday. What became apparent to me after I got clean and sober was that the very need to (try) to control my drinking and using was indicative of my addiction. I was constantly having to fight the impulse to binge. And, the truth is, many times I failed to control myself, lapsing into drunken blackouts, vomiting, driving drunk, and all the other associated behaviors of alcoholism and drug addiction.

For this exercise share with someone or write down all the ways that you tried to control your addiction, whatever it was, and all the ways that you failed at control. As you talk about this, also talk about how it felt to be trying to control yourself. This again points us to the craving, the obsessiveness, and the powerful effect of our addiction on our emotions and mind states and reminds us of the suffering we caused ourselves by succumbing, over and over, to these impulses.

Exercise: Triggers

What triggers your addiction(s)? These may take many forms. Explore these topics in relation to what creates craving in you, what sets you off on a binge, or what has caused you to relapse:

- **Relationships** – for many of us, difficult family or intimate relationships are a big trigger.
- **Social life** – if you socialize with drinkers or druggers, it's going to be very tough to avoid drinking or using.
- **H.A.L.T.** – "Hungry, Angry, Lonely, Tired." Do you get into any of these states before you relapse?
- **Work** – work stress is a big trigger. At the end of a long day or week it can feel as if we "deserve" to have a drink.
- **Loneliness** – isolation and loneliness are common to addicts and alcoholics. That's one reason why meetings are so important.
- **Moods** – sadness, anxiety, and anger are common triggers for using. Most addicts and alcoholics have a hard time facing their emotions. A vital part of recovery is learning to be with emotions without reacting, doing something destructive or self-destructive.

Once you've acknowledged your most common triggers, ask yourself how you can avoid them. Some are easier than others, but if you are really committed to your recovery, you'll find a way.

Step One

"We admitted we were powerless over alcohol (drugs, food, sex, gambling, people, etc.), that our lives had become unmanageable."

What's this Step About?

The language of Step One, especially the idea of being "powerless," can distract us from what the Step is really about: quitting. As much as the Twelve Steps and Buddhism are spiritual practices, they are both founded in action, in behavior. And the starting point of that behavior in the Steps and in recovery is to stop doing what we've been doing. This is the simple function of this Step, to change our addictive behavior so that we can start the work of recovery.

I also find it useful to view Step One as the beginning of a process, the archetypal spiritual journey. The journey starts in darkness, a "bottom," that wakes us up to the unworkable nature of our lives as we've been living them. Just as Buddhism starts with insight into suffering, recovery starts when we honestly confront our own pain. This may be as simple as a persistent cough triggering the thought, "I'll never see my grandkids grow up if I don't quit smoking," or as dramatic as waking up from a blackout in a prison cell—and not knowing why you're there. No one can tell you what your bottom is. I've been amazed over the years of my recovery to see how little it sometimes took to push someone over the line into a program, or on the other hand, how resistant someone could be to recognizing their need for help even when everything in their life was falling apart.

Yes, Step One is about Powerlessness and Unmanageability, but both of those things are meant to motivate you to quit.

Exercise: Living Powerlessness

Living powerlessness is true surrender. It means keeping awareness of your lack of control in the forefront of your consciousness. An essential part of maintaining recovery is remembering powerlessness—not just over your addiction, but over many other things. When we get into a struggle with things we can't control, we can trigger the kind of frustration and stress that leads to relapse.

Start by contemplating the range of things you are powerless over: people in your life like parents, children, employer, friends, etc; your own aging and illness; the weather, the traffic, the economy. The list goes on and on.

Remember powerlessness in your daily life when your car breaks down or you get a parking ticket; when you don't get the job you want or the deal at work falls through; when you don't get what you want, whatever it is.

Powerless Over Thoughts and Feelings

Perhaps the most difficult issues around powerlessness are our thoughts and feelings. "Cheer up," people will say, or "Think positive!" And sometimes it's possible to do these things, but often it's not. Our thoughts and emotions are the result of past experiences, traumas, and conditioning; of habitual patterns, deeply embedded in our psyche; of familial, cultural, and genetic causes. All of these causes *are in the past*, and therefore we are powerless over them. The only thing we have power over is *the present moment*. The key then is how we *react* to the thoughts and feelings that arise.

The starting point is realizing that thoughts aren't necessarily true and that feelings aren't necessarily giving us accurate information. When I first experienced depression as a teenager, I felt as if I couldn't do anything, so I didn't do anything. I sat (or lay) around bemoaning my miserable state. And guess what? It got worse. Only years later did I realize that the feeling that I couldn't do anything was not true, and that, in fact, if I continued to do the things that I normally do, like show up for work, friends, and my spiritual practice, that the depression would tend to pass much more quickly.

I can't make the feelings not come, and I can't make them go away. They seem to have a life of their own, which is why I categorize them as something I am powerless over.

The same seems to be true of thoughts. Sometimes the awful, hateful, negative thoughts just flood in. The important thing for me is to have at least some inkling of a perspective that asks, "Is this thought really true? Is it useful? Is there another way of looking at things?" This last question is essential and often a lifesaver. I tend to interpret many experiences as about me. "Only five people came to my class tonight. I guess people don't like me." Whereas, maybe it was the rainy weather or the holiday weekend that kept people away.

The same applies when it's a sellout. Maybe people aren't there because I'm so great, but because the topic I explore is of interest to them.

Since we often can't know if a thought is really true, it's wise to keep watching.

Meditation: Powerlessness and Surrender

Start by practicing Mindfulness of Breath as shown in the Introduction.

As you practice, notice how, even though you are trying to pay attention to the breath, your mind keeps wandering. There may be a tendency to try to control this, to force the mind to stay with the breath. However, instead of this route, I suggest that you do the opposite: just let the thoughts come without pushing them away. They won't stay long if you don't struggle with them.

Imagine that your mind is very spacious, that there's lots of room for thoughts, feelings, sounds, and sensations. Surrender to all that is coming through your mind. Feel your breath, but don't cling to it. Notice thoughts, but don't follow them. Feel sensations, but don't recoil from them.

Just let everything come and go without trying to control it. Stay attentive to all this, not just spacing out, but watching with interest.

See if you can find the balance between making an effort and letting go. This is the sweet spot of meditation.

* * *

Many people in 12 Step programs portray the transition from active addiction to being clean and sober as somewhat magical. This ties in with the God-related Steps and culture of the program, and conveniently fits into a story of redemption, kind of like the song "Amazing Grace": "I once was lost, but now I'm found; was blind, and now I see." The narrative goes something like this: "I was lost in my addiction, stumbling blindly from one binge to another, from one selfish and destructive action to another, but then God opened my eyes and struck me sober." I understand the impulse to describe what happened in this way because the change from drinking and using to being clean is so stark that it can seem as if there is no connection between the two. But if this is how it works, it leaves people who are outside—people who want to get clean and sober but don't know how to—in a somewhat hopeless and helpless position; apparently there's nothing they can do but wait for God's grace to *maybe* descend on them and strike them sober. Or else, they are left feeling that if they could just *believe* enough in God, then they'd be taken care of. For many people who have no belief in God, this is an untenable situation, and potentially cause for despair.

And I believe that this description of recovery is seriously flawed, and in fact, represents, what in Buddhism would be called "delusion." The Buddha teaches the Law of Karma: that all actions have results, and that all results have causes. Therefore, getting sober must have a cause. To think that recovery is a magical process denies the Law of Karma. Further, I believe it disempowers us. If we don't have a part in getting ourselves sober, then we are at the mercy of unseen forces that might turn on us and decide that we should drink. Ouch!

Of course, this makes no sense, and one of the things that I ask people to do in their recovery work is to trace back the karmic actions that resulted in their recovery. Let's do that now.

Exercise: Tracing Back Recovery

Write a brief narrative history of your own skillful actions *before recovery*. These can be related to your recovery, like trying to stop drinking, switching from hard liquor to beer, cutting out hard drugs, limiting use of drugs or alcohol (or binge foods, pornography, gambling, whatever your addiction) to certain times (e.g. weekends) or situations (like being with friends). Skillful actions can include aspects of your lifestyle, perhaps your work is service-oriented, you were a good and loyal friend, or you stuck to certain moral principles, even when using.

This can also be related to your spiritual path. Many people are pursuing a spiritual or religious path concurrent with their addiction. These things and many others (be creative!) can all be part of the thrust of causes that eventually result in recovery "magically" happening "all of a sudden."

When you've finished this narrative, read it and try to take in that you weren't a bad person who got good, but rather that part of you was always trying to do the right thing. From a karmic standpoint, we could say that up until the transition into recovery, the power of our addictive actions was greater than the skillful ones, but at that point—and for some people this transition is an awkward one full of fits and starts—the skillful actions and intentions finally reached critical mass, and you transitioned into recovery.

Of course, this is just a model, and life rarely fits so neatly into our models. Nonetheless, I believe it's important to take credit for our positive actions just as we must take responsibility for our negative ones.

The Four Noble Truths and the Practice of Recovery

To understand the connection between Buddhism and recovery, we can look at the core teachings of the Four Noble Truths and how they correlate with the 12 Steps.

The first time the Buddha taught anyone after his enlightenment, he explained the Four Noble Truths. Throughout his teaching career, he repeated this teaching, expanded on it, and used it as a model for understanding many other ideas. What's interesting is that this teaching follows a traditional Indian medical model: diagnosis, cause, prognosis, prescription. In that sense it fits with the idea of healing that recovery implies.

The Noble Truths address the fundamental questions we all have: "Why is life so hard, and what can we do about it?" The Buddha called this the problem of "dukkha," a word that is typically translated as *suffering*, but whose meaning is nuanced and subtle, perhaps better understood as "unsatisfactory," that is, there's no point in life where we arrive at permanent satisfaction. When we begin to practice meditation and discover the complex layers of inner and outer challenges in our lives, or simply in life, the meaning of *dukkha* unfolds and becomes clearer.

Perhaps I can summarize the Four Noble Truths this way: (1) While some elements of life are inevitably painful, like getting sick, getting old, and dying, (2) many of the difficulties we experience are created by our own tendency to crave pleasure, avoid pain, and cling to that which can't be held; (3) nonetheless, if we see these Truths and how they work, it's possible to break the pattern and achieve happiness and freedom; (4) the way to achieve this freedom is by following a practical set of guidelines for life and spiritual practice.

When listed in their traditional form, the Four Noble Truths are somewhat cryptic and enigmatic. Entire books have been written explaining them, and if you are interested in Buddhism, you will want to explore them in other contexts.

1. The Truth of Suffering
2. The Truth of the Cause of Suffering
3. The Truth of the End of Suffering
4. The Truth of the Way to the End of Suffering.

In my analysis, the First and Second Noble Truths relate to Step One and the Third Noble Truth to Step Two. The Fourth Noble Truth which encompasses the Noble Eightfold Path can be seen as that which we "turn our will and our lives" over to, as Step Three suggests, but its comprehensive nature applies to many of the Steps, so I'll spread it out over various Steps that seem relevant.

The First Noble Truth: Suffering

In the fall of 1964, when I was in 9th grade I began to struggle with my emotions. Feelings of sadness and despair crept up on me. I'd come home from school, and instead of studying or going outside to play, I'd collapse on the couch and stare at the ceiling. My interest in school lapsed and I lost my appetite. I was depressed.

I felt helpless, that I couldn't function, and that there was no point in trying. Because I believed those feelings, I gave up trying to function. My parents became deeply concerned and sent me to a psychiatrist. I talked to him, but never understood what our conversations were supposed to achieve.

In the spring my mood lifted again, and I got through the school year okay. Unfortunately, the next year I wasn't so lucky. Another episode of depression and despair culminated in a bout of mononucleosis and my failing 10th grade. The following year I dropped out. I tried twice more to finish high school, but failed, ending up getting a G.E.D. at nineteen.

It was during these dark times that I also discovered drugs and alcohol. Dependence quickly developed out of my feelings of despair and emptiness, and for the next nineteen years, I lived the life of an alcoholic/addict.

When I look back at those early bouts of depression, one thing stands out for me: I didn't understand that I could *feel* helpless, but not *be* helpless. I didn't realize that what I was experiencing was the pain of life, and that I didn't have to succumb to it. I didn't understand the First Noble Truth, that life is hard.

Today I still have bouts of depression, but I don't lie on the couch staring at the ceiling. I carry on.

I was raised in a privileged environment, and like many people, my parents tried to protect me from life's challenges. That was an act of love, but it had a fatal flaw: I didn't learn how to live with life's challenges. What I had to face at fourteen was hard. Depression is difficult at any age in any situation. But I had no tools for living with those feelings. I thought, "If I feel as if I can't function, then I can't function." In the Twelve Step world, they say, "Feelings aren't facts," but nobody told me that when I was fourteen. As far as I was concerned, my feelings were giving me vital information: "You can't do anything, and there's no point anyway." So I gave up.

Further, because I'd come to expect that everything in life should be rosy and I should always be happy, the only activities I pursued were ones that I enjoyed, namely, playing music, and later, drinking and drugging.

For me, coming to understand the Buddha's teachings on suffering has been vital in learning a different way of relating to life's difficulties. Realizing that difficulties, both inner and outer, are a natural part of life, helps me to accept the challenges that come. When I expected everything to be easy, difficulties completely overwhelmed me. But when I began to understand that things aren't always going to go that way, I started to be able to weather the obstacles.

The Buddha says that the appropriate response to the First Noble Truth is to *understand* suffering. For the addict, this means seeing your addiction, and this idea is embodied in the first of the Twelve Steps: "We admitted we were powerless over alcohol (addiction, drugs, food, sex, people, etc.), that our lives had become unmanageable." This Step expresses our understanding of our addictive suffering, and thus begins our recovery process. Until we see suffering, there is no possibility of change.

When we constantly avoid pain or difficulties, we are constantly in conflict with reality. Hiding from pain, denying our failings, ignoring suffering, all of this requires a lot of energy, and must ultimately fail. Accepting difficulties is a freeing surrender; seeing suffering evokes compassion; opening to the truth brings wisdom. The Buddhist path is not about imagining a perfect world or even trying to create utopia, but rather seeing the truth clearly and responding skillfully and kindly to what you see.

Exercise: The Truth of Suffering

Be careful when doing this exercise not to indulge in morbid self-reflection. This is just the first part of the Four Noble Truths. We have to see suffering clearly first before we can treat it. Try not to take what you uncover personally, and remember that the rest of the Four Noble Truths will help you to deal with the suffering you find in this exploration. This exercise has three parts:

1. **Your challenges**: write a list or narrative of the real life difficulties you face. These can range from health issues, to relationship and family problems, work problems, and financial problems. It can include chronic emotional difficulties like depression, bipolar, or anxiety conditions. The gist of this part of the exercise is that you are looking at the difficulties that just come with being a human. While you may have some influence

over them, you're essentially not in control, or at least, right now, you don't see how you can control them.

Seeing this list should break any denial you have about the Truth of Suffering. It's important, though, to see your problems in the larger context of the dharma, that is, to see that they aren't personal or unique to you. As you go through the list, consider all the other people who share the same forms of suffering. You are not alone in your difficulties and pain. You are simply experiencing human life.

2. **Your attachments**: in this part of the exercise, probe the ways in which you create or exacerbate your problems through clinging or rejecting. These may be related to your challenges. For example, if you are having financial problems and, instead of trying to deal with them in practical ways, you spiral into despair, you are making the problem worse. Here we are trying to separate the *reality* of the problem from our *reaction* to it.

3. **Your addiction**: while this obviously falls under "Your attachments," it's important to highlight the specific ways in which your addiction causes you suffering. Look at all the ways your drinking or drugging, your codependence or your enabling, your eating or your sexual relationships—or *all of the above*, have created suffering in your life. In the 12 Steps, this is your Step One inventory, a review of your history with your addiction. Consider all the ways your addiction has caused you and others pain: emotional, physical, financial, and spiritual. Here we must emphasize honesty. The tendency of addicts is to downplay the harm we've caused. If you are going to get into and stay in recovery, you *must* face the full effects of your addiction.

Note: Be careful that "honesty" doesn't turn into self-recrimination. Guilt is a useless emotion, and it's always about the past. Try to review your addiction without creating more suffering for yourself.

The Second Noble Truth: The Cause of Suffering

When I woke up on June 7, 1985, it was over. I knew I couldn't drink or take drugs anymore. The night before, my pickup band had been fired from a cheesy gig in the suburbs of L.A.; I was at the end of a six-month run on drinking, drugging, and cheating on my girlfriend. I finally was able to face the fact that *I* was responsible for the direction of my life. No longer could I blame the music business or my parents, my girlfriend or even my emotions: it was my responsibility to create the life I wanted, no one else's.

I was thirty-five then, and I'd been struggling since I was fourteen, trying to figure it out. But there'd always been this blind spot: seeing how my grasping for pleasure and avoiding pain had led me to avoid responsibility. I'd never been willing to face my own flaws or to do the uncomfortable work of self-examination, and so I'd always slid along the sidelines of my problems, never going straight in.

The most obvious way that I avoided dealing with life was by staying high. This never seemed like the biggest issue for me—I mean, I was trying to be a rock star; I was dealing with depression; I couldn't keep a relationship together; and I was living in poverty. All that stuff seemed more significant than my daily diet of pot and beer, the things that helped me to get through, or so I thought.

But finally, in my despair, I was willing to try one last thing: stop drinking and using. That turned out to be the foundation for change.

I wanted to get the results—fame, riches, happiness—but I didn't want to take the time to do the foundation work. Like all addicts, I wanted instant gratification. And by addressing the basic grasping for pleasure that was my addiction, I actually started to address the broader issues of effort, patience, and building towards a future that depend on *delayed gratification*. While my addiction was a real problem in and of itself, it was also a metaphor for my whole approach to life: give me pleasure now, without effort. When I gave that up, it allowed me to see how I brought that attitude to all of my life, from my relationship with my girlfriend to my aborted education to my stalled music career. All of it had suffered from my unwillingness to deal with challenges.

Fundamentally, that day I had realized the Buddha's Second Noble Truth: *dukkha* is caused by craving and clinging. It's our constant longing for things to be different from the way they are that creates our lack of satisfaction, our sense that things are never right. Of course, this is the essence of addiction—craving and clinging to our drug of choice—and another aspect of Step One, that what makes our lives unmanageable is our desperate attempt to satisfy every craving. Not only is our addiction causing us all sorts of problems, but it's central premise, that getting loaded will bring some satisfaction, is false. No desire can be satisfied because everything is impermanent: as soon as you satisfy one craving, another arises, which is why we go on using or drinking or acting out over and over, grasping after an unreachable end to craving.

To me the key concept in this truth is that the reason we struggle isn't because of the way things are, but because of our *relationship* to the way things are. If I can accept things as they are, I don't struggle, even if things are difficult. If I can't accept things, then the slightest variance from my own preferences is upsetting. When we practice mindfulness meditation, we are watching this process unfold moment by moment, and that's an important part of meditation, to see how you react to thoughts, sounds, feelings, sensations, and the whole range of experience. We see very quickly the first and second Noble Truths, the inherent discomfort in existence and our desire to change that.

The Buddha goes further in defining the cause of suffering when he says that, besides clinging to pleasure, clinging to identity is our problem. For me, this was true on many levels. I clung to the idea of myself as a musician: that's who I was and that's all I could do. This held me back from exploring any other career and imprisoned me in the dead end of bar gigs. I also clung to the idea of myself as depressed: that's how I was and there was nothing I could do about it. This held me back from any healing and furthermore, from taking responsibility for change. These fatalistic beliefs crippled my life.

It is this whole range of clinging, from sense pleasures, to emotional states, to ideas of who we are that causes suffering. In recovery, we face all these demons. Dropping our long-term habits and addictions doesn't end clinging. In fact, for many of us, removing the obvious addictions only reveals the tendencies beneath them, and we discover that we cling and cause ourselves suffering in all kinds of ways. And many of us find that absent our comforting drink or drug, we seek other pleasures that can be similarly destructive, overeating, sex addiction, smoking, shopping, or gambling. Barring such obvious problems, subtler forms of obsession, controlling, or aversiveness may appear.

The Buddha said that the wise response to the Second Noble Truth was to *abandon* clinging. Ultimately, that is the task of all spiritual work, and the task of a lifetime. Our meditation practice, and the entire Eightfold Path are just about this single task.

Exercise: Letting Go

There are many approaches to letting go of those things that cause suffering, and that's what most of the exercises in this book are about. These exercises are a mix of traditional and contemporary approaches.

1. **Let go:** go down the list from the "Truth of Suffering" exercise, and ask yourself how you relate to each issue. If there is aversion or desire, any grasping, rejecting, or clinging, associated with an issue, see if you can understand how that relationship of non-acceptance is causing you suffering. This is actually how we end suffering, not by ridding ourselves of problems, but by accepting the problems without being in conflict with their reality. Try, even if just for a moment, to let go of your aversion or desire and see how that feels.

2. **Replacing with the opposite**: for example, sending thoughts of lovingkindness to our enemy. In the 12-Step program, we say, "If you have a resentment, pray for that person." The purpose of this isn't to do something to make that person's life better, but to ease your own heart, to let go of the painful feeling of anger and resentment. Another example is you might try to replace anxiety with calm by doing a concentration exercise.

3. **Observe your own suffering**: when you bring mindfulness to the clinging itself, sometimes you'll let go naturally. If not, you will at least be seeing clearly how you are creating your own pain. Eventually you may give up.

4. **Observe impermanence**: when we see clearly how everything is in constant flux, we are more likely to let go, since it becomes obvious that nothing actually can be held for long. This approach to practice emphasizes careful investigation, one of the key

elements of insight meditation practice. Investigation doesn't mean *thinking* about what is happening, but rather observing closely and seeing if we can perceive closer and closer the details of experience and begin to detect patterns and processes within experience.

5. **Deepen concentration**: peace and stillness have a natural "cooling" effect that eases our clinging. Our hearts soften, our emotions grow calm, and that to which we cling can fade away. Look at some of the concentration practices offered in the "Building Concentration" section of Step Eleven.

Exercise: The Desire Beneath the Desire

Oftentimes, beneath our surface desire is something more basic and primal. In this exercise, we'll try to see what underlies the obvious desires. This is a one-on-one exercise.

Explore the question, "What was/is the desire that my addiction was/is trying to satisfy?" Keep drilling down with every answer until you feel as if you've gotten to something fundamental and authentic. Take at least five minutes for each partner to answer. The partners do not respond to each other during the formal practice, but simply create the safe space for each other to look within.

For the "non-addict," the question might be "What longing in you never seems to be satisfied?"

In doing this exercise you keep "drilling down" for a deeper answer. As in the TV show "Who Wants to Be a Millionaire?" we keep asking, "Is that your final answer." Is there a question you can ask about this answer?

Step Two

"Came to believe that a Power greater than ourselves could restore us to sanity."

Step Two presents us with the first reference to God in the Steps, here characterized as "a Power greater than ourselves." The capital P let's us know we're serious now. If you have issues about God, as so many who come to my teachings do, this is the first button that gets pushed in the Steps. How are you doing to deal with that? I know a lot of people just say, "I can't do the 12 Steps," or they simply won't try a 12 Step program because they see the word God. That's fine if you are actually going to try to deal with your problem in another way, but often this winds up being an excuse to *not* deal with the problem, whether it's drinking, drugging, or something else.

There are some who have developed programs that intentionally avoid any reference to a Higher Power, and I think that's great. I've chosen instead to "work within the system" of the 12 Steps. My belief or philosophy is that every path of recovery, and indeed every authentic spiritual path, must contain some basic elements common to all, and so what I'm interested in discovering in the 12 Steps is those fundamental components. And one of those components, it turns out, is trust or faith in the process itself as well as in our own capacity to achieve a spiritual awakening. In Step Two we are confronted with this question of faith or belief.

What's This Step About?

When I first read the 12 Steps I thought Step Two was saying, "If you just believe that God will fix you, the power of your faith will take care of everything." This was a very Christian reading of the Step, which might very well have been its original meaning. I was willing to suspend disbelief and skepticism and play along—"God? Sure, why not?" That worked for a while. I kept doing the grunt work of recovery, everything from showing up at meetings, being of service, and writing inventory to getting a day job, going back to school, and starting to deal with my relationship issues. There was a feeling of magic that everything seemed to be falling into place, all those little "God shots" and synchronous moments. People kept showing up just when I needed them—teachers, employers, friends—and it all seemed to be happening because I "Let Go and Let God."

That's one way of looking at it. And there's nothing inherently wrong with that way of looking at it. Maybe. . .

Today I see Step Two in completely different terms. First of all, the way I understand it now is that the Step is saying, "There is hope. It is possible to change. Things can get better." The reason that statement is important is that when you're an addict, you don't think you can change. In fact, that's the whole point—you want to stay loaded all the time—you don't want to change. One of the reasons it's so hard to take Step One, to actually quit drinking and using, is that the question that looms in the background is, "What then?" How are you going to deal with not drinking? We have the sense that our life is going to be the same, only worse because we won't have the relief of getting high. Why would we choose that? The whole reason we are getting loaded all the time is that we don't want to be in our life as it is. Step Two is offering us an alternative; it's saying that there's a completely different life out there for us.

Okay, but the Step says "a Power greater than ourselves." Just believing that it's possible to change and for your life to get better doesn't seem to involve some big power. But, if we think about it, for anything to happen, some power or force or energy has to be involved. To get out of bed, a lot of muscles have to be involved. To take a midterm exam, a lot of study and thinking have to be in play. Nothing happens without power. And the power of intentional change is the power of karma. Actions have results; that's what the Law of Karma says. Drink and use all the time, and the result is addiction. Stop drinking and using and the result is being clean and sober. When we take Step One and stop, that's essentially what we're doing, using the Law of Karma to establish ourselves in recovery.

If we don't believe we can change, if we think we are bound to stay addicts forever and that we can't heal, then we don't believe in the Law of Karma. We are saying, "No matter what actions I take, I am fated to be a suffering addict." From a Buddhist viewpoint, this is called "delusion," or Wrong View. It means that we don't understand the way the world works. We believe in fate, that everything is preordained and we have no power to do anything about it. Nonetheless, most of us, when faced with the question, "Do my actions have any effect on my life," will say, "Yes, of course." The Buddha said that if our actions didn't bring results, he wouldn't bother teaching people because there would be no way for them to achieve enlightenment; they wouldn't be capable of change.

But this belief that we can't change is implied in the despair of the addict who can't seem to stay sober or feels stuck in negative emotional or behavioral patterns. That's why it's important to take Step Two, to confront this, often unacknowledged, belief consciously and see how we are being held back by our delusion. Once acknowledged, we can begin to consciously build a belief system. We can start to ask ourselves, "What do I need to do to change and grow?" Then we can begin to access the powers at our disposal, powers like love, determination, awareness, wisdom, the support of others, and, yes, faith. Whether we know it or not, as addicts we've been using powers, but mostly negative ones like selfishness, impatience, fear, and resentment. Recovery means working with the positive powers. The faith or belief involved in Step Two is when we "come to believe" that it's actually worth changing our behavior and orientation. Once we believe that change is possible and that it's worth making the commitment to a new way of living, we are ready for Step Three.

Exercise: I'll Be Okay

Do this exercise with a trusted person. Say to your partner, "I'll be okay, because. . . " and then give a reason why you'll be okay now that you are in recovery. Your partner should say, "Yes, you'll be okay. What else?" And then repeat, "I'll be okay because. . . " and give another reason. Continue for about five minutes or until it feels complete.

An alternative approach is to exchange statements. In this method, one person says "I'll be okay because. . . " and the other responds, "Yes, you'll be okay." Then the second person says, "I'll be okay because. . ." and so on, back and forth.

At the end of the exercise, state and recognize, "And right now I am okay."

Exercise: Stop Fighting

If you have struggled with whether you want to go into a 12 Step program; with the idea of God; with "those people" in meetings; with your own ability to succeed in recovery, what if you just stop fighting? What if you put this all aside, and any other objections or resistance and just surrendered to the process?

Consider any ways you have been resisting the recovery process, whether they are about the program or about you or your beliefs, and ask yourself if it might be possible to simply drop that resistance, if only for today. Question yourself and your beliefs. Don't believe everything you think.

Exercise: Stop Trying to Control Everything

Start to notice all the ways that you try to control the world. How do you try to get others to do what you want them to do? How do you try to control your own feelings and mind states, with or without intoxicants? How do you rebel against being told what to do or being controlled by others?

Ask yourself what would happen if you didn't try so hard, if you just let go.

Watch your thoughts, words, and actions today and see how many of them relate to controlling things, whether it's traffic, your job, your family, your health, your mood, or anything else. Notice the subtle and not-so-subtle ways that these efforts cause stress, frustration, anger, and suffering.

See what happens when you let go of these efforts for a moment. Breathe, release, relax.

Exercise: Karma and Change

The way your life unfolds is fundamentally related to your past thoughts, words, and deeds. This is the Law of Karma. How your life unfolds in the future is founded on your present moment thoughts, words, and deeds.

Therefore, change is possible. To believe otherwise is delusion. Not only that, but change is inevitable, this is the Truth of Impermanence. How things change in your life is largely dependent on your thoughts, words, and deeds.

Ask yourself if you hold conscious or unconscious beliefs that go against these truths. Do you sometimes feel as if things are unfolding in a way that you have no effect on? That life is random? That you are fated to suffer these things? Does it seem as though you can't change? That you are stuck in your addiction or your negative patterns in work, relationship, and emotional states? Remember that you can take actions today that will change your life for the better. Remember that even when it seems as if you are stuck, that you are always in transition, that things will inevitably change, and that if you continue to do the right thing, they will change for the better.

Whenever you feel stuck, reflect on these ideas. This is your contemplation.

Exercise: Why I'm Not God

Many people coming into recovery and looking at the 12 Steps have a fear of losing control. They have the sense that if they aren't running things, who will? That it's not safe to let go. To counter this feeling, if you have it, consider all the mistakes you've made in your life.

Start with your addiction and the mistake of letting a substance or behavior take over and damage your life. Consider your romantic relationships and the mistakes you have made there, whether in choosing inappropriate partners, treating people poorly, cheating, giving up, avoiding intimacy, and all the other ways we undermine our relationships. What about your education and professional life? Have you made mistakes and failed in those realms? And how about your ideas and beliefs? Have you always been right?

Seeing all the ways that you have made mistakes in your life, acknowledge that if you were God, or even if you just had it all together, you would never have lived this way. Obviously you aren't God; obviously you need help; obviously you should open to the possibility of doing things another way.

Exercise: Is There Help?

When I give workshops at treatment centers, I like to point out to people that just by being there they are acknowledging a "power greater than themselves," that they have taken a Second Step. By showing up, paying money and following the program, they are saying that they believe that they can get help—"be restored to sanity"—by the center. Even if they don't believe in God, they do obviously believe that something outside of themselves, in this case, the treatment center, its staff and program, can be of help.

Ask yourself what help there is for you in your life. It might be the 12 Steps and its members; a therapist; a spiritual teacher; a book or workshop; your family or friends. Is there some strength or wisdom inside you that can help you? Some experience or knowledge you can draw on?

There is help everywhere, in the breeze blowing, in the warmth of the sun, in the children we see at the park. There is help within and without, if we just open to it and let it in.

The Third Noble Truth: The End of Suffering

The Buddha's teaching on cause and effect, the Law of Karma, says that if suffering has a cause, then if we undo that cause, we can end suffering. Thus, if clinging causes suffering, letting go brings relief. This Truth tells us that freedom is possible if we let go. In the Twelve Step model, this is Step Two. While the third Noble Truth doesn't mention a power, by holding out the hope of change, it expresses the same idea as Step Two, that we're not stuck forever in the round of suffering or in our addiction. Just this realization itself has a freeing effect.

The Third Noble Truth and the Second Step both relate to the awakening of faith on the path. This isn't a religious or blind faith, but rather a trust in a process that, while it appears to make sense, we haven't fully experienced yet. When we come into a 12 Step program, we see that it's working for others, even though we haven't yet gotten the benefits; this can give us enough trust to try. In the same way, when people come to a Buddhist meditation class or retreat for the first time, they see a bunch of people who seem to be benefiting from the practice.

The Buddha said that the wise way to respond to the third Noble Truth is to *realize* it. When we realize that suffering and addiction can end, we are inspired to stick to the path.

Exercise: Do You Believe?

One thing that undermines all effort in recovery and spiritual growth is lack of faith, faith in the path and faith in our own ability to succeed on the path. For this exercise, explore these two questions:

1. **Does recovery work?** Do you think that your path of recovery is effective? Whether drawing on 12 Steps, Buddhism, or some other approach, does it seem to work for you and others? See if you can fully take in the truth that recovery is possible.

2. **Can you do it?** Do you believe in your own ability to get into recovery and stay in recovery? Especially if you've relapsed before or if you've lacked discipline in your spiritual practice you may lose faith in yourself. Do you understand that you are capable *in any moment* of making the right choice? No one is inherently flawed to the point that they can't get into recovery or develop a meditation practice. If you have an embedded belief

that you can't change see if you can recognize that in many cases, this is simply a belief, not founded in fact. The key is to *take the actions necessary for change.* **Try this exercise:** choose one issue that troubles you about yourself, and today do one thing differently from your habitual way of behaving, either internally or externally. Stick with this for a week and see what happens.

Exercise: My Spiritual History

Step Two often brings people face to face with their existing beliefs, or lack of beliefs. From the Buddhist perspective, all beliefs are conditioned, that is, they are formed through past experiences. Depending on how we were raised, the beliefs that were inculcated in us from childhood, the encounters we've had with religion and religious people, our own personal tendencies, and many other factors, our beliefs are formed.

In this exercise, I'm going to ask you to deconstruct those beliefs, to explore all the factors you can uncover that contributed to forming your present belief system. In this way, I hope that you will become a little less attached to your beliefs, understanding that they don't represent some absolute truth or even, perhaps, the most logical conclusions about reality, but that they are the result of all these causes, and can thus be questioned and even abandoned if they are not serving you or if they are built on shaky foundations.

In this exercise, I suggest that you write down or share, chronologically, the major influences on your spiritual beliefs. You can start by writing down the beliefs you were raised with; then explore how those beliefs changed as you got older. Many teenagers start to question the religious beliefs of their childhood. Look at any spiritual explorations that you've taken in your life, either through study, reading, or practice. Look at your *rejection* of beliefs as well. Keep your idea of what is "spiritual" very broad. One friend realized that his experiences with LSD were actually important spiritual transitions. Others find that their beliefs

84

about money, relationships, and even politics reflect something essentially spiritual.

When you get to the end of the exercise, look back over this history and consider whether the beliefs you have today are necessarily true or whether you can be open-minded about what you believe, especially as you move forward in recovery. It's vital, if we want to continue to grow, to remain open to possibilities. Our addiction is a static place, inflexible and incapable of change. Only if we are willing to question our beliefs will we be able to stay free.

Step Three

"Made a decision to turn our will and our lives over to the care of God, as we understood Him."

What's This Step About?

Step Three sounds as if it's about God, but from the perspective of the archetypal journey, I think that's a very limited view. Instead, I think it's about making a commitment to a new way of living, to living in harmony with the Law of Karma, with the Dharma.

First of all, making a decision, *any decision*, for an addict is progress. We don't "decide" to get drunk, crash the car, and wind up in jail; we don't "decide" to binge or overdose or waste our lives. These are impulses, obsessions, addictions. So when we actually make a decision, that is, consider alternatives, make a choice, and act on it, we are already showing progress.

In Step Three, the decision we are making is to turn away from our previous addictive, self-centered, pleasure-seeking way of living, and turn towards something more healthy, spiritual, and ethical. If we're approaching this process from a Buddhist perspective, a big part of this Step is to engage the Noble Eightfold Path, which I'll talk about later in this Step.

Turning "our will and our lives" over is about two things: setting our intention to live differently, "our will," and actually taking the action, "our lives." This distinction in the Steps corresponds to the Buddhist understanding that all actions follow on the heels of intention. If we are *trying* to do the right thing, we are already in better shape. We may succeed or we may not—we may even relapse—but if we are clear about what we really want, we'll be able to get back on track. Intention, as I'll talk about later, conditions the results of our actions, that is, if we do something for the right reasons, the results will tend to be beneficial; if we do them for the wrong reasons—selfishness, pleasure-seeking, resentment—the results will tend to be unbeneficial.

So, this Step is about setting our direction and trying to stick to it. It becomes our touchstone. Finally the Step implies acceptance. If we are "turning it over" to something else, whether God or the Dharma, we are saying that our job is to show up and do our best, but that we don't control the results. Therefore, we need to learn to accept how things unfold. A lot of the problem with the addictive personality is the effort to control everything, and when we can accept how things are occurring in our lives, there is much less conflict and turmoil, less stress. We come to see that, even if things don't turn out exactly as we wanted, they are workable. And many times, what we thought was a "bad" result, turns out to have hidden benefits. Many times in my recovery I found that in the longterm, disappointing results led eventually to a much better outcome than the one I had wanted. This is what "turning it over" is about, and it's key to maintaining serenity in recovery.

Exercise: Acceptance

The Big Book of AA says famously:

"And acceptance is the answer to all my problems today. When I am disturbed, it is because I find some person, place, thing or situation -- some fact of my life -- unacceptable to me, and I can find no serenity

until I accept that person, place, thing or situation as being exactly the way it is supposed to be at this moment."

What does this mean to you? How true is it for you? What about things you don't think you *should* accept?

How much does *lack of acceptance* cause agitation, stress, and suffering in your life?

Begin to notice things you have difficulty accepting:

- What is difficult to accept in your past?
- What is difficult to accept about the world?
- What is difficult to accept about yourself?
- What is difficult to accept about your experience during meditation?

Dharma God

Using Buddhist teaching and practices in a 12 Step context necessarily forces us to confront the "God question." I've written a whole book on this topic, *A Burning Desire: Dharma God and the Path of Recovery*, so if you're interested in seeing the extent of my thinking, that's the place to find it. Nonetheless, I want to sketch out some of the basic ideas.

To start with, we can recognize that the Dharma is powerful. If "God" represents a power greater than human individuals, one that we must deal with one way or another, then the Dharma fulfills that meaning. Here are some excerpts from *A Burning Desire* that encapsulate some the elements of the Dharma and the power that they have:

- **The Law of Karma** - This brings results from actions based on the moral fabric of the universe. It is the force behind addiction, recovery, and spiritual growth. We use this power to transform ourselves and our world through intentional thoughts, words, and actions.

- **Mindfulness** - This is the power of attention and non-reactivity. It opens us to wisdom and insight through clear seeing. Mindfulness is the foundation of all spiritual growth as it reveals the truth of the way things are, internally and externally.

- **Impermanence** - This is the energy of change that continuously transforms us and our world. Engaging this power helps us see through the illusion of solidity, showing us the futility of clinging and the frailty of life. Insight into impermanence inspires us to let go and to deeply engage life as it is in each moment.

- **Love** - This is the underpinning of caring, generosity, and service that holds people together. The power of love weakens self-obsession and reveals our interconnectedness. It is the source for joy, compassion, and fulfillment.

While Step Three says to "turn your will and your life over" to God, another way to think of it is to "live in harmony with the Dharma." That means we are turning away from our addictive and self-centered way of living towards a more skillful set of principles and powers. Living in harmony with the Dharma means that we ask ourselves whether our thoughts, words, and deeds are in accord with these ideas. Inevitably this will mean thinking, speaking, and acting differently.

So, for example, we might ask ourselves, "Am I being mindful?" or "Is this a loving act?" This then helps us make more skillful choices.

Exercise: Your Higher Power Today

Share with a friend or spiritual mentor what your conception of Higher Power is. Or, if you don't have a conception or are atheist or agnostic, share your sense of no Higher Power.

Commitment

Commitment to a life clean and sober is a vital aspect of maintaining our recovery. If we are going to do this successfully it's going to mean more than a casual effort, but a whole lifestyle change. This can mean new friends, new hangouts, new ways of spending free time, even new employment. It's difficult to stay clean if you are hanging out with all the old friends who are still getting loaded. Further, "turning your will and your life over," means more than not using: it means living a life of integrity and morality. People who are successful in their recovery are honest, generous, and compassionate. They don't lie, they aren't promiscuous, and they don't steal or cheat. Many of us wanted to be good people, but under the influence we acted on our lower impulses. Now that we have dropped our use of intoxicants, we find it easier to live a clean life in all respects.

Exercise: Commitment – Values

Ask yourself what you are committed to in your recovery. What are your values? How do you want to live now? How do you hold back from absolute commitment to recovery? What loopholes do you still have?

Exercise: Commitment - Practice

For meditation to be most effective, we need to practice regularly. Make a commitment to meditate for a certain period of time each day.

Exercise: Commitment - Taking Refuge

Taking Refuge is a traditional Buddhist form of making a commitment to your spiritual path. There are three elements of Refuge: Buddha, Dharma, and Sangha.

Refuge in Buddha – Buddha represents the enlightenment principle, the germ of awareness inside us all. In simpler terms, it means being mindful, so taking Refuge in the Buddha can simply mean that we are committing ourselves to living as mindfully as we can today.

Refuge in Dharma – the Dharma is the Truth. It also means the teaching of the Buddha. When we take Refuge in the Dharma we are committing ourselves to living in harmony with the Truth. Another way of thinking about this is that we commit ourselves to viewing all our experiences today through the lens of Dharma instead of the lens of "I." This commitment then requires that we actually study the Dharma so we know how to look at things.

Refuge in Sangha – Sangha is the spiritual community, the people who are committed to a path. In the recovery world we call this "the fellowship." When we take Refuge in the Sangha, we commit ourselves to being engaged with our spiritual community. This means that we will try to help others, and we will go to the community for help for ourselves. We will do service for the community and the individuals in the community.

You can take Refuge in a formal ceremony in some traditions. It's also very helpful to take Refuge on a daily basis, reciting the phrases, "I take refuge in the Buddha; I take refuge in the Dharma; I take refuge in the Sangha" and reflecting on their meaning.

Exercise: Holding Back

- How do you hold back from fully committing to your Buddhist practice?

- How do you hold back from fully committing to your recovery program?
- Make a vow that counters these forms of resistance.

Faith and Turning It Over

Although Buddhism isn't considered a "faith-based" religion, it nonetheless requires faith to practice fully. Just to commit time in your day to sit silently, essentially "doing nothing," requires a certain amount of faith that there is benefit in meditation. When we sit through physical or emotional pain, it's because we have faith that there is a value in working with these challenges. When we sign up for a 10-day meditation retreat for the first time, it takes quite a bit of faith.

In the recovery world, we talk more about faith. We learn to take actions whose results we can't control because we come to realize that our job isn't to control things, but to show up and do our best. Naturally we want to know that we're going to get the results we want, but wisdom tells us that this isn't realistic. In our addiction, we always wanted things to be to our liking, and to get what we wanted. This grasping is what led us to keep taking drugs and alcohol that "guaranteed" a certain result.

Now we learn to do our best and let go. Step Three frames this in terms of "God," but in fact, a belief in God isn't necessary to begin to live with the wisdom of turning it over and letting go.

Exercise: Turning It Over

- Have you really turned "your will and your life" over to something in your recovery? Are you committed to living a life of integrity?

- What is difficult for you to "turn over"? What is easy? What could you do to make it possible to turn more difficult things over?
- What do you take refuge in that is less wholesome?

Practice: Making a Vow

As part of your daily meditation, **make commitments or vows** that correspond to your "decision" in this Step. These can be based on the Five Precepts or you can just make them up.

For example:

"Just for today, I take the **Training Precept** to refrain from using intoxicants." Then you can list triggers, such as: "Just for today, I will avoid going to a bar or liquor store; just for today, I will avoid other alcoholics or addicts who are using."

You can do these practices around any issue, food, sex, relationships, speech, love, or resentments. Be creative. When we regularly contemplate things like this, it helps us to become more established in our commitments.

It's important, even with these vows, to include **forgiveness** when we slip or fail.

The Fourth Noble Truth: The Way to the End of Suffering

The Fourth Noble Truth is the path the Buddha taught for moving towards freedom, and in the Buddhist model, enlightenment. Because the teachings were originally an oral tradition, and possibly because the Buddha had a very systematic mind, this teaching is also preserved as a list: The Noble Eightfold Path. I will address certain elements of the Eightfold Path in this chapter, Step Three, and some in other chapters. My understanding is that each of the elements of the Eightfold Path is powerful and can thus be a part of our Higher Power:

1. Right View – seeing the Law of Karma and the Four Noble Truths
2. Right Intention – aiming toward kind, wise, and skillful actions
3. Right Speech – speaking what is true, kind, and timely
4. Right Action – following the Five Precepts of Non-Harming
5. Right Livelihood – working with the intention of service
6. Right Effort – letting go of the negative, cultivating the positive without striving
7. Right Mindfulness – bringing clear awareness to all experience
8. Right Concentration – calm abiding, clear focus

It's important to note that when we say "right" in this context, it doesn't have a black and white or right and wrong meaning, but something more akin to the sense of being in tune or in harmony with each of these elements.

The Buddha said that the wise response to the fourth Noble Truth was to *cultivate* it. That means, we need to act on these principles. Here the proverbial rubber meets the road. As Bill Wilson points out in his commentary on the 12 Steps, *Twelve Steps and Twelve Traditions* (aka *The 12 and 12)*, this emphasis on action is inherent to the 12 Steps.

When working with Buddhist teachings, the Dharma, this means that we start to try to live our lives by the principles of the Eightfold Path (as well as other Buddhist teachings). It's a Buddhist principle that it is up to the individual to move their own spiritual progress forward by acting on spiritual teachings and practices, and both the Eightfold Path and the 12 Steps give us frameworks for this process.

For some, the idea of a path that is founded on our own action excludes the concept of God or Higher Power. For me, there's no difference. Turning my will and my life over to the Eightfold Path is the same process as turning it over to God. In neither case am I expecting God to fix me or solve my problems. Really what I'm doing is trying to live in harmony with God, or in the case of Buddhism, with the Dharma. Either one is a relinquishment of ego, or preferences and reactivity, a turning toward a set of wise, guiding principles.

The Noble Eightfold Path is less a linear process than a matrix of interlocking, interwoven elements. Some of these elements have very particular instructions—Right Mindfulness, Right Action—while others are simply pointing to an attitude or understanding—Right View and Right Intention. There's no simple or mechanical way to practice or understand these teachings, which is as it should be for a set of ideas that is meant to take you to the ultimate level of human consciousness, Nirvana. If it were simple, if it were easy, it wouldn't be ultimate.

Given the multi-faceted qualities of the Eightfold Path, it's wise to take a multi-faceted approach to its practice. For Right View and Right Intention, we'll be working mainly with contemplations and reflections; for Right Livelihood, Speech, and Action, we're more involved with daily life and our interactions with others; and with Right Effort, Mindfulness, and Concentration, the focus is meditative. This approach accomplishes several things: it brings these teachings into every facet of our lives, much as Step Twelve suggests that we "practice these principles in all our affairs"; it gives a variety of approaches to our recovery work so that those with different needs and at different stages of this work will be able to relate to and use at least some of these practices; and finally, it cultivates many different aspects of our spiritual practice, giving us a well-rounded and integrated recovery practice that leads us to wisdom and spiritual maturity.

Right View

Right View means that we are seeing reality as it is, not through the filter of our own fantasies, illusions, views or opinions. For the addict, this is coming out of denial and seeing how crippling our dependence is. Further, Right View makes the connection between clinging and suffering that the Buddha shows us in the Second Noble Truth. Another important aspect of Right View is seeing the impermanent nature of all phenomena, external and internal. All of this amounts to a practical view of the world. The Buddha wasn't a mystic, but rather was trying to understand life in its most basic elements: why it's difficult and how we can make it manageable and ultimately satisfying.

Exercise: My Delusions

This exercise is best done with a partner or group. Giving feedback is encouraged. Honestly look at the delusions you continue to cling to. For instance:

-   I can still drink and/or use.
-   If I just meditate and pray enough, God will take care of me.
-   I'm in control.

- I have no control.
- I'm responsible for everything.
- I'm not responsible for anything.

What other delusions do you hold? Try to look beneath your behaviors to see patterns that reveal "delusion."

Right Intention

Once we see the truth with clarity, Right View, we are motivated to change, Right Intention. This motivation is the key to our ongoing recovery process and spiritual development. While we may continue to make mistakes or even relapse, a strong intention will keep us on track, eventually bringing us back to the path.

When I first learned to meditate, my goal was peace and some kind of magical spiritual fix. For two years I did a Hindu practice mechanically, just sitting and repeating a mantra for twenty minutes twice a day. Not much happened, and I believe that the problem was my intention. I wasn't committed to a real spiritual awakening; I just wanted meditation to make my problems go away.

When I then discovered Buddhism, I think my intention started getting closer to something skillful. I began to see the process as broader than just taking a "meditation pill." But I still couldn't acknowledge the depth of change needed, and I lacked the willingness to address those fundamental issues.

From the time I started that first meditation practice until I got sober was seven years. That's how long it took for my intention to become clear and strong enough for real change to happen.

The 12 Steps and the Eightfold Path aren't mechanical processes. We don't just go through a series of actions to get a desired result. We aren't just *acting* differently; we are becoming different people. Intention is at the heart of this change.

Initially, most people who work the 12 Steps go through them as a linear process, admitting they are powerless, working with the Higher Power idea, inventorying and then trying to let go of failings, making amends, and doing service. For many people this is an important exercise and one that helps to solidly establish them in their recovery. But simply going through the process isn't enough. If it were, more people would be successful in their recovery. What the process is trying to accomplish is what Step Twelve calls a "spiritual awakening."

I used to think the Buddhist parallel to this was enlightenment, but that term has so many meanings in different traditions and contexts, that I don't find it specific enough. What seems like a clearer comparison is what's called a "transformational insight," an insight that changes who you are, how you respond, and how you behave in the world. While many insights may occur as the result of spiritual practice, only *transformational* insight actually changes you for good. And the underlying quality that transformational insight changes is your intention, that which motivates and gives purpose to your thoughts, words, and deeds.

(Of course, enlightenment is supposed to be transformational, but given the number of supposedly enlightened Buddhist masters who drank alcoholically or acted inappropriately in their sex lives, it calls into question the use of the term.)

It's important to understand why the Buddha said that "karma is intention." While the typical understanding of karma is that actions bring results, what the Buddha is saying is that what *motivates* the action is what determines the quality of the results. This means that following a simple mechanical process—like the Steps, like the Eightfold Path—isn't enough for transformation. The spark of motivation must be there or the process will be hollow and ineffective. This is, of course, a good protection against hypocrisy.

This idea, though, seems to come up against the 12 Step idea that we need to "act our way into right thinking, not think our way into right action." This suggests that we should "fake it till we make it," another popular 12 Step idea. This goes back to people trying to think their way out of their addiction instead of just stopping using. The 12 Step program, then, is thought of as more behavioral than psychological. Nonetheless, if we look closely, we see that intention, or as the Steps talk about it, "willingness," is essential for change to happen. We see this in Step Three, which says we turned our *will* over to "God." We see it in Step Six, which says that before we can change we must "be entirely ready." And we see it in Step Eight, which says once we'd made a list of those to whom we needed to make amends we "became willing to make amends to them all." Obviously the Steps are asking us to do more than simply take action; they require us to change the heart of those actions, our motivations. No matter how many times we go through the mechanics of the Steps, until we become people who want to be sober; until we become people who want to live with integrity; until we become people who want to be loving, compassionate, and wise, we will never establish solid recovery.

Exercise: My Intention

Intentions are rarely pure. Few of us are motivated solely by greed and hate, or by generosity and love. When considering your own intentions, try to look with balance and compassion. That means, don't be too hard on yourself, but don't be too easy. Of course, only you can determine that balance.

1. Begin by considering what the motivations were that led to your addiction. Explore the search for pleasure and the avoidance of pain; the selfishness and self-centeredness; the delusions and confusions. Next, remember the positive motivations you had, even when lost in your addiction. Think about the ways you were kind or a good friend; the longing you had for spiritual connection; the ways you might have developed a talent or worked hard; and your desire to overcome your addiction.

   This first exercise is meant to help you see the mixed nature of your intentions--neither perfectly evil nor perfectly good—and how your positive intentions eventually led you to recovery.

2. Now make a list of your short and longterm goals. Include everything from your commitment to recovery, to relationship, work, and spiritual goals. You can get quite specific, like committing to a certain number of 12 Step meetings each week and a certain amount of meditation each day. After you have the list, go through it one-by-one and ask yourself what the intention behind these goals is. Is it self-centered or service-oriented? Is it based on getting pleasure and comfort, or wisdom and serenity? Ask yourself, "What kind of person do I want to be, and what do I need to do to be that person?"

3. Finally, make the commitment or vow to follow your positive intentions to the best of your ability; to keep them in mind when making decisions; and to return to these intentions when you realize that you've strayed.

PART TWO: INVESTIGATION AND RESPONSIBILITY

Steps Four through Nine take us into the gritty work of recovery, looking at our failings, our past transgressions, our habitual thoughts, words, and behaviors. Starting with the Fourth Step Inventory, we are now into the real work of change. This requires both rigorous honesty and a willingness to let go. But this work allows for a great renewal in our lives, healing our relationships, letting go of limiting ideas about ourselves, and opening previously unimagined possibilities. While we'll need great courage to pass through the fires of these Steps, great rewards will come.

Step Four

"Made a searching a fearless moral inventory of ourselves."

What's This Step About?

If Step Three actually worked the way it sounds as if it did, that is, if you could really turn your will and life over to the care of God, then it would be the last Step. God would take care of everything else. Ironically, not only is that not the case, but the following Step is one of the most challenging of all. Why should we have to produce this moral inventory after turning everything over to God?

In fact, what I think happens in Step Three when we "make a decision" to change is that we're forced to face all the things that *need* to change. We see that it's not so easy to just "turn it over." Step Four, then, begins the actual work of change.

In a sense, Step Four is an inventory of our karma, our past actions and intentions. The later Steps put us to work on those issues.

Step Four, is included in Right Mindfulness. With mindfulness we are exploring ourselves and exploring the Dharma. In our self-exploration, we honestly face our failings as well as our positive qualities. Mindfulness, both inside and outside of formal meditation practice, allows us to see our habitual thought patterns, our opinions, and our emotional habits. While mindfulness has been called "radical acceptance," I think that it is also "radical honesty," an intense inner looking that, when engaged authentically, can't help but reveal our so-called "character defects" and "shortcomings." This self-examination is an ongoing aspect of both the Steps and the Buddhist path.

Right Action

Buddhism is known in the West as a meditative tradition, but the way we live, our morality, is the underpinning of meditative development. Without integrity and kindness, any spiritual work is simply froth with no substance. Right Action involves following the Five Precepts, which in characteristic Buddhist fashion are described as "trainings" rather than rules or commandments. In this sense they are guidelines for living, signposts to which we orient our behavior.

When I first encountered the Precepts, I thought of them as secondary to mindfulness and concentration and of course to my ultimate goal, enlightenment. Once I got sober, though, I realized that my inability to live even by such basic moral principles had crippled, not only my meditation practice but my spiritual and emotional development. I realized that I needed to go back to the beginning, the basics of Buddhist teachings and rebuild the foundation of my practice. The Precepts continue to be not only guidelines for me, but contemplations, as I reflect each day on my behavior and how it affects others, the world, and myself.

Investigating the Precepts and their role in our lives brings us up against our understanding of the Law of Karma. I personally shy away from formulaic interpretations of this law, like direct retribution for specific actions. I also don't take a stand on the idea that in some future life I'll reap the reward or punishment for an action in this lifetime. It's not so much that I reject these ideas, as I view them as things that I can't know, while more obvious results of karma are knowable. It's these evident karmic resultants that I'm interested in because I clearly can do something to affect them.

For example, when I explode in anger, the karmic results are evident here and now: the person I get angry with likely strikes back or is hurt; I feel the immediate pain of the heat of anger in my body; and I quickly feel remorse and regret for losing control. I don't have to get into any mystical beliefs to see the truth of this connection.

It may be more exciting to think that if I give a dollar to a homeless person I'm going to win the lottery, but this kind of magical thinking tends to blind us to the more obvious results of our actions: giving feels good and it helps others. Is it possible that there will be other karmic results from a gift? Sure, but it's unlikely we'll ever really know.

In the traditional texts, the Buddha says that there are long-term karmic effects from our actions, but that we don't have to believe that. He points out that, even if all we consider is the karmic effects "here and now," we'll be motivated to follow the Precepts. That seems like a sensible approach.

In the larger sweep of a lifetime, we can see the karmic patterns play out more clearly. Decades of drug, alcohol, food, or tobacco abuse take a toll on the body and mind. Even if we get clean, those effects may follow us. On the other hand, those things that we devote ourselves to also bear fruit. When I began meditating at 28, I didn't do it with the idea of teaching and writing books. I was following an inner compass that pointed to the value of spiritual development. Thousands of hours of meditation later, I got the opportunity to share my experience.

When I began to study creative writing in my first year back at school—just three years sober and trying to find a new path in my life—I certainly didn't plan on applying my skills to a book on Buddhism and the 12 Steps. But thousands of crumpled up pages later, that's what arose. These tracks, of meditation and writing, were passions I followed, not Precepts. But they expressed the positive side of the Precepts, the heart's longing for connection and creation. When we engage in the study and practice of Buddhist morality, we are seeking out the best way of living, the best way to develop and share our gifts with the world, and to overcome our self-centeredness, grasping, and confusion.

Exercise: Taking The Five Precepts

The Precepts are sometimes called, "The Five Precepts of Non-harming," This points to their essence. What's important isn't so much the specifics of each Precept, but rather the spirit of non-harming. Rather than seeking a narrow interpretation of a rule, socially engaged Buddhists try to broaden the meaning of these Precepts.

1. **To refrain from killing any living being**: Reflect on the meaning of this precept for yourself. Some people take it to mean they should be vegetarian, and, although Theravadan Buddhism doesn't require this, many Buddhists feel it's an appropriate way of expressing this precept. You might also expand the meaning of "killing" to include other ways of harming, such as political suppression, physical abuse, or harming nature. Does adherence to this precept mean that you must oppose all war? Allow pest infestations of your house? Or, as some sects do, filter your water carefully to avoid killing microorganisms? You can see that the precept isn't so simple when you start to explore it carefully. Just remember that the Buddha's path is

called "The Middle Way," so be careful of pursuing extremes that make no practical sense. As we say in the 12 Step world, "Progress, not perfection."

Many of us have been wounded—literally and figuratively—in war, abuse, and other violence. Many of us have wounded others in the same ways. Part of taking this precept is exploring our responsibility and wounds from our experiences of violence.

Begin to bring more mindfulness to your relationship with all beings and see if you can be non-harming.

2. **To refrain from stealing or taking what is not ours**: Reflect on the meaning of this precept for yourself. There are obvious ways in which we want to follow this precept, and for many addicts and alcoholics, that is an important step in the right direction. We certainly want to bring integrity to our work life, as well as our family and social life. We might also consider ways in which we "steal" things like time and attention. Is cutting someone off on the freeway "stealing"? At one 12 Step meeting a young man shared that part of his "program" was to return the shopping cart after he'd put his groceries into his car. I thought that was a perfect example of the level of mindful integrity that both Buddhism and the 12 Steps foster.

Begin to bring more mindfulness to the ways you try to take from others and see if you can create less grasping.

3. **To refrain from sexual misconduct, that is, from hurting others through our sexuality**: Reflect on the meaning of this precept for yourself. For many addicts, sex is an underlying addiction, if it isn't our primary one. Many of us acted unskillfully when intoxicated. When we get into recovery, we may be faced with something we've never done before: sober dating. Our culture gives such mixed messages about sex that it can be

difficult to know what's right. On the one hand, many movies and TV shows depict sex as something that happens as soon as two people find themselves attracted to each other. Besides that, many of the images in the media are designed to trigger sexual desire. At the same time, religions preach abstinence, anyone caught acting inappropriately is vilified, and no seems to be able to convey what might be a "normal" or healthy sexuality.

Early in my recovery my sponsor suggested that I make a commitment not to sleep with someone until I'd really gotten to know them and established a relationship. This meant at least a half-dozen dates, probably more, over the course of maybe six-to-eight weeks before sex. For me this was a radical suggestion. I'd been used to the idea that if I liked someone and they liked me, we should sleep together. If that didn't happen relatively quickly, then I assumed we weren't "meant" to be together. Of course, that strategy hadn't worked too well in my romantic life. Changing my approach to relationships was one of the most important parts of my recovery, and eventually led to the most stable and long-lasting relationship of my life.

There are other elements of our sexuality that bear attention. It's said that Internet pornography is the "crack of sex addiction," and this is an issue for many (especially men) in recovery. This is another issue that is very personal, but it's wise to talk about it with a sponsor, therapist, teacher, or trusted friend. As with any potential addiction, we have to be rigorously honest about our behavior. Is it hurting me? Is it hurting others?

Our sexuality affects more than strictly sexual activities. We can bring our sexuality into social and work situations in inappropriate ways, flirting, dressing provocatively, or misusing power relationships. Obviously, the appropriateness of flirting depends a lot on our relationship status. We need to be careful, though, whether we are trying to manipulate people with our sexual attractiveness. In the same way, a boss, teacher, or therapist can sexually manipulate those working or studying under them.

Our sexuality is a part of us, whether a celibate monk or a sexually active college student. We need to bring care and mindfulness to the ways we project and act on our sexuality in the world. Sexual desire is so powerful that the Buddha said that if there were another form of desire so strong, no one would ever become enlightened.

Begin to bring more mindfulness to your sexuality and see if you can act more skillfully.

4. **To refrain from speaking what is not true**. Reflect on the meaning of this precept for yourself. When we start to apply the principles of Right Speech, we discover the challenge of speaking the truth, the fundamental question being, "How do I know this is true?" A lot of what we believe and what we say is overstatement or opinion. For instance, I used to say, "I'm always depressed." This, of course, was not true. I was expressing the way I felt sometimes, but I wasn't really thinking about whether it was factually true. And, the power of speech is such that saying something so negative has a very negative effect on my mood, making it somewhat self-fulfilling.

Opinions often show up as comments about what someone else should do or why something happened. When I say, "You shouldn't do that," I'm stating an opinion, and, in most cases, I simply don't know if that's true. Similarly, when I say, "He drinks so much because his mother was an alcoholic," I'm making a claim I simply can't back up. With simple variations, we can make the same points without stating absolutes: "I don't think you should do that," is more accurate, and more helpful, I think; "I wonder if his mother's drinking is behind his problem," states my opinion while admitting that I really don't know.

Begin to bring more mindfulness to your speech everyday and see if you can speak the truth more often.

5. **To refrain from using alcohol or drugs that cause us to be careless or heedless**: Reflect on the meaning of this precept for yourself. The Fifth Precept is one of the direct connections between Buddhism and recovery. It points to the value of sobriety and being drug- and addiction-free on a spiritual path. For anyone (such as myself) who has ever tried to meditate when intoxicated, you know the fruitlessness of such efforts. But, of course, this precept goes much further than just saying you shouldn't try to meditate when you are drunk or stoned. I personally have come to see being clean and sober as a sacred state in and of itself. What I mean is that facing each moment of my life in this unfiltered way creates a continuous clarity that is precious to me. Wisdom is something that takes time and clarity to develop, and when I interrupt my clarity with intoxication, it brakes up any accumulating wisdom with a kind of trauma.

We can think of intoxication beyond drugs, as well. Things like TV, the Internet, smart phones, and many other things can act as numbing agents on our hearts and minds. As part of this precept, it's often suggested that you consider whether your use of media is undermining your mindfulness. Investigate any activities that over-stimulate, numb, obsess, or intoxicate you. It's not that we're trying to cut out all pleasurable activities, but rather, become aware of the ways in which they might be holding back our spiritual progress. Relaxation and down time is important. We just don't want it to dominate our time and energy.

Begin to bring more mindfulness to the ways that you avoid your feelings through substances or activities.

Exercise: Five Precepts Inventory

Review your past behavior in relation to the Five Precepts:

To refrain from killing any living being - Rather than just being about killing, I think it's helpful to look at all forms of violence. How have you been physically violent or emotionally abusive? How did your addiction tie into this?

To refrain from stealing or taking what is not ours – Look at any ways you have stolen, whether obvious or not-so-obvious. This can include skipping out on work or not paying back a loan from your parents. Mostly it's about the ways we cut corners and try to get over on people. Recovery is about integrity in all aspects of our lives.

To refrain from sexual misconduct, that is, from hurting others through our sexuality – For some addicts, this was their "drug of choice," but even if you don't identify as a sex addict, you probably have issues. Many of us acted out sexually when we were intoxicated. Many of us were selfish in our sex lives or used our sexuality to manipulate others. For many in recovery, trying to learn how to be skillful in our sexual relationships is the hardest thing after getting sober/clean itself.

To refrain from speaking what is not true – This precept is really about how we use speech generally. Besides lying or misleading, do we gossip, swear profusely, or habitually speak in destructive or negative terms? Do we interrupt or try to keep the focus on ourselves? Do we give unwarranted advice? Do we actually listen to people?

To refrain from using alcohol or drugs that cause us to be careless or heedless – If you are already clean and sober, the question becomes, what other things do you use to avoid being present and feeling your feelings? The list is long including, technology (Internet, smart phones, TV, music); food; sex; gambling; sleep; exercise; work; and general busyness.

For each of these precepts, consider both your past behavior, its ties with your addiction, and the ways it harmed others, and your present behavior and whether you are living up to your spiritual values. You can do this exercise as a personal written exercise, as one-to-one sharing, or in a group, if people feel safe with that.

The Five Hindrances

The Five Hindrances are the typical difficulties and challenges that arise during meditation and in our lives. Unlike the "character defects" referred to in the 12 Steps, they are not personal or unique to us, although the way they manifest will be individual. Nonetheless, the understanding of the Hindrances is that we shouldn't take them personally.

In a sense, mindfulness meditation is an inventory of the Hindrances, at least much of the time. When we sit in meditation we are often attacked by these energies and the way we respond to those attacks will largely determine both how much we enjoy our meditation and how deeply we go with it. In Step Seven I'll talk about working with antidotes to the Hindrances. For Step Four, I'm going to suggest that you simply get more attentive to the arising of the Hindrances and how they affect your practice and your life.

Here are the Five Hindrances:

- **Desire** - The prime cause of addiction, desire is the longing that tells me that if I can just get the next thing or experience or feeling, then I'll be okay; I just need a new car, a new job, a new relationship; I just need a drink, a drug, a meal; a vacation, better weather, deeper meditation. The problem with desire is just what the Buddha pointed out: whatever

111

we're after, it's never enough. We get the new car and it gets a scratch; the new job requires being away from our family; the new relationship is great—for a while, and then it's like all the other relationships we've been in. We have a drink and we want another; we go on vacation, spend too much and wind up homesick. This is the nature of *dukkha*. Because everything constantly changes, no solution is permanent, so it's an illusion that the next thing will bring satisfaction. We can have moments of pleasure, which is fine, but none of them will last. Furthermore, if we explore with mindfulness the feeling of desire, we'll discover that desire itself is somewhat unpleasant, even when it's simply a minor wish. When it turns into craving, it is truly painful, and it's not surprising that it drives us to act in unwise ways.

None of this is to say that desire is "bad." Desire is perfectly natural, and no matter how much we meditate or deepen our spiritual life, we'll likely experience some kind of wanting. Desire is fundamentally driven by our survival instinct, and without it we'd probably be in trouble. Buddhism isn't so much about *getting rid* of desire as it is to *change our relationship* to desire. This means that we see desire clearly; we see how it causes suffering; we see how it arises and how it passes; and we aren't driven to act by every desire that arises. We become more conscious of how desire is affecting us and make wiser choices about which ones we act on.

- **Aversion** – The flip side of desire, aversion is the other primary cause of addiction, the wish to get away from how we feel. Aversion takes many forms, anger, resentment, depression, fear, irritability, impatience, and just plain not liking the way we feel. The essence of aversion is that this present experience is not acceptable. There's a sense of urgency, "I've gotta get out of here," with aversion. This urgency tends to blur our judgment as our need to change our situation or mental/emotional state pushes us to act without carefully considering the possible results or alternatives. When we're caught in these painful states, we're susceptible to our addictive cravings because we just want to escape. Aversion, then, is one of the most dangerous triggers for relapse.

The unpleasant nature of aversion makes it even more difficult to explore than desire. Not only do we want to get away from the feeling, but we certainly don't want to explore it. Nonetheless, as with desire, a conscious effort to be with aversion will expose its nature as painful, impermanent, and lacking personal identity. When we see clearly how it is controlling us we will likely be motivated to let go or at least find another way of working with the feeling we're having.

- **Sloth and Torpor** – Probably the most common question I get in my meditation workshops is "I keep falling asleep; how can I deal with that?" While people seem to think this is a "meditation problem," I actually think that it goes beyond meditation. Sometimes people seem to forget that when they sit down to meditate they are using the same body and mind that they live with. In our culture we somehow seem to expect that we can work 80 hours a week, run marathons, stay constantly connected online, commute for hours every day, and then be able to sit down and meditate with a bright and relaxed mind and body. Instead, our meditation experience is just a reflection of the activities we do outside of meditation. If we work all the time we'll be exhausted when we meditate, and probably spend the whole time thinking about work. If we don't get enough rest, we'll be sleepy; if we're worried, we'll worry; if we're angry, we'll be angry. Meditation, rather than an escape from our lives is, in some ways, just a mirror of our lives. In that sense, our practice can be an inspiration to change our lifestyle.

Nonetheless, there are ways to work with sloth and torpor in meditation. (The antidotes can be found in Step Seven.). First, we need to become aware of our tiredness and what it feels like. This is, in some sense, counter-intuitive since being sleepy means we are shutting down our awareness. In our meditation practice, first we just want to catch the arising of tiredness as early as possible so that it doesn't overwhelm us. Then we want to use mindfulness to explore the sensations associated with tiredness.

Besides the physical aspect of this hindrance, the mental one is also challenging. People who are slipping into fatigue often find their meditation to be very pleasant, as dreamy images and thoughts start to arise and the body relaxes deeply. Unfortunately this is usually a sign that you are falling asleep. If you start having random, dreamlike thoughts, you're probably in sloth and torpor and should use some of the antidotes.

The more troubling aspect of the mental side of this hindrance is the dull mind of depression. A negative, aversive tone pervades the thoughts, and we have very little energy to counter them. It's hard for us to think clearly, and the mind seems to be stuck in a rut. It's vital that we recognize these states and work against them. Otherwise, we just sink into despair.

Sloth and torpor also has a direct relationship to our addiction as acknowledged in the acronym HALT, Hungry, Angry, Lonely, *Tired*. Fatigue or tiredness is a trigger for addiction because our usual defenses are weakened and the tiredness gives us a feeling of longing. Alcohol masks fatigue, which is one reason people go to the bar after work, and many people are addicted to stimulating drugs like cocaine and amphetamines. Other people actually seek out low states of energy with opiates and barbituates. Clearly this seemingly benign state of sloth and torpor carries hidden risks for the addict.

- **Restlessness and Worry** – Restlessness and worry is the flip side of Sloth and Torpor. In this state it's difficult to even sit still, and the mind spins out. The physical aspect is a sense of energy in the body, a need to move, change position, get up, walk, do anything but sit still. This, of course, makes sitting meditation very difficult. Nonetheless, sitting still is perhaps the best way to work through such energy.

The mental aspect of this hindrance is the obsessive focus on a single worry. The mind keeps spinning with anxiety but never comes to any resolution. These thoughts intermingle with the physical anxiety of restlessness to create a pervasive sense of fear and loss of control. The extreme version of this is a panic attack. Mindful breathing, conscious relaxation, and deepening concentration are powerful ways to work with this challenging energy.

Addicts often talk about wanting to "get out of their own skin," which is an expression of restlessness. When we feel this way it's important to recognize that we are being triggered. The tendency with Restlessness and Worry is to immediately act. Restlessness is a trigger for impulsive behavior, and so it's vital that we see its nature and catch it before acting unwisely.

- **Doubt** – Doubt is the most subtle and dangerous hindrance because acting on it can result in relapse or giving up our spiritual practice. Denial of our addiction is a form of doubt, and many people relapse when they decide they aren't really addicts or alcoholics.

Another form of doubt is questioning our own ability to stay clean and sober. For people who have repeatedly relapsed this is especially prevalent. It's natural to start questioning yourself when you've failed over and over. It's remarkable to me, though, how many people I have encountered who struggled terribly in their early efforts at recovery, but are now firmly established with years of time under their belts. Nonetheless, if we have strong doubts they are going to make it even more difficult to hang in through the early stages of recovery.

Another form of doubt is when people think they are no good at meditation. This is very common for beginners, especially if they think that they are supposed to turn off their thoughts in meditation, a common misconception. It takes a certain amount of faith in the meditation process and in ourselves to stick it out through the challenging early stages of learning meditation.

Meditation: Labeling Desire and Aversion

In order to truly know and understand desire, we must observe it in our minds and bodies.

Begin by doing the Mindfulness of Breath exercise from the Introduction.

Whenever you notice that your mind has wandered, check what you were thinking about and see if there is a quality of desire or aversion in the thought. Most times you'll find there is.

Make the mental note "desire" or "aversion" depending on what you observe.

Notice how your body feels now and if there is any emotional charge or physical stress or tension anywhere in the body. Often thoughts of desire and aversion trigger these uncomfortable feelings. They may be very subtle or more obvious. Take a moment to feel those physical and emotional sensations, then come back to the breath.

Every time your notice your mind wandering, check again what quality is in the thought and note it. And each time, return to the body to see the results of the thought.

Continue this observing and returning for at least 20 minutes. Notice if, during that time, there is any change in thoughts, any increase or decrease of desire and aversion.

117

Meditation: Inventory – Five Hindrances

- **Desire** – During meditation, start to notice when you are having a thought of desire. Notice how that desire feels in the body and mind.

  In your daily life, notice when the desire to act on your addiction arises. Breathe, relax, and don't act on the craving, just feel it in your body. Then, notice when the desire has gone away.

  Further, start to notice how desire runs other daily behaviors. Try to become more aware of the arising of desire before you act so that you can make wiser choices about what desires to act on.

- **Aversion** - During meditation, start to notice when you are having a thought of aversion. Notice how that aversion feels in the body and mind.

  In your daily life, notice when aversion triggers addictive craving. Breathe, relax, and don't act on the craving, just feel the aversion in your body. Then, notice when the aversion has gone away.

  Further, start to notice how aversion runs your daily behavior. Try to become more aware of the arising of aversion before you act so that you can make wiser choices about what aversions to act on.

- **Sloth and Torpor** - During meditation, start to notice when sleepiness or dreamy, dull thoughts are arising. Notice how that feels in the body.

  In your daily life, notice when sloth and torpor triggers addictive craving. Breathe, relax, and don't act on the craving, just feel the fatigue in your body. Then, notice when the fatigue has gone away, or else, take some action, like a nap or rest.

  Further, start to notice how you use and abuse your body's energy in your daily life, how stress, overwork, over eating, unhealthy eating, and overstimulation sap you. Try to become more aware of the arising of sleepiness or fatigue before you act so that you can make wiser choices about what energies to act on.

- **Restlessness and Worry** - During meditation, start to notice when you feel restless or your thoughts are spinning out. Notice how restlessness feels in the body.

  In your daily life, notice when restlessness and worry triggers addictive craving. Breathe, relax, and don't act on the craving, just feel the energy in your body. Then, notice when the restlessness has gone away, or else, take some action to release the energy.

  Further, start to notice how restlessness drives your daily activities. Try to become more aware of the arising of restlessness and worry before you act so that you can make wiser choices about what energies to act on.

- **Doubt** – During meditation, start to notice went doubting thoughts arise, and start to question their validity. Notice if you are doubting your own ability to meditate or the value of meditation itself.

  In your daily life, start to notice the doubts you have about your addiction. This is a good time to review your Step One and remind yourself of all the ways that your addiction harmed you and others.

  In your daily life, start to notice how your own self-doubt undermines you; and start to notice how cynicism or skepticism weakens your ability to fully commit to wide ranging aspects of your life, from work to relationships, from challenging situations to playful activities. When we are stuck in this form of doubt, we are always holding something back from our lives, from ourselves, and from the people around us.

Meditation: Labeling

This meditation builds on the previous one. It is a variation of a practice that's usually associated with the Burmese master Mahasi Sayadaw, and is usually called "Noting" practice.

Begin as usual by settling into a comfortable, alert meditation posture and starting to focus on the breath. Once you've established awareness of the breath, begin to notice thoughts as they arise.

Each time you realize that the mind has wandered from the breath to a thought, make a soft mental note of "thinking, thinking." Do the same with sounds, labeled "hearing, hearing," and sensations, labeled either "feeling, feeling," or "sensation, sensation." The words themselves aren't so important as long as they point clearly to the experience.

Once you become familiar and comfortable with this practice (and this might take several sittings, or perhaps you'll be ready right away) start to refine the labels you give to thoughts. This means that you might notice a thought of "planning, planning," or "judging, judging," "remembering, remembering," etc. The idea is to see the quality or type of thought you are having. You might find yourself saying "work, work," or "vacation, vacation." I often hear music in my head which I simply label as "song, song."

After a while you'll probably notice patterns that you hadn't recognized before. This practice can give us great insight into our own minds. And as we develop this deeper awareness of our habitual and automatic thought patterns, we may be able to let go of some of these thoughts, becoming less the victim of our negative or destructive subconscious beliefs and obsessions.

Exercise: Inventory – My Positive Qualities and Actions

For many of us it may be even harder to look at our positive qualities than our negative ones. There are two reasons that I think it's important to do a "Positive Inventory": one is that it's simply not true that all of our behaviors were negative, so a negative inventory is a limited and inaccurate view of reality. The other is that the Fourth Step inventory can be depressing; it can give us a very negative feeling about ourselves that can undermine our recovery. Many addicts already have a painfully negative self-view, and if the inventory simply reinforces that it's not helping.

For many of us, this can be a difficult inventory. Sometimes we may feel that we don't have any positive qualities. Or we might feel that it's arrogant or egotistical to talk about our good side. If we've been persistently criticized as children or stuck in self-hatred, this process might seem alien. Take care with this exercise, really watching the things that show up. If there are obstructions, make those the focus of the exercise until you can get by them.

If you're doing the exercise with a partner, notice comparing and judging mind. Maybe they seem full of themselves, or maybe you don't feel you measure up compared to them. These are all ways that our thinking undermines us. Notice those thoughts and try to let them go.

Contemplate, share, or write on topics such as this:

- **My positive intentions** – What kind of person do I want to be? Do I want to be kind, generous, and wise? Do I try to be loyal, helpful, and compassionate? Do I want to work hard and contribute to the world? Remember that just having a positive intention is karmically significant. It's our intention that motivates our actions, so having positive intentions is the foundation for being a better person. Give yourself some credit for at least *wanting* to be more skillful in your actions. We can't always do the right thing, but having a good intention is a start.

- **My friendships** – What positive qualities do you express in your friendships, such as loyalty, compassion, helpfulness, or simply being a good listener?

- **My relationships** – Even if your intimate relationships haven't worked out, did you bring any positive qualities to them, being loving, supportive, or generous? Consider ways you have been a good partner to your lovers.

- **My work** – Have you been a good employee or worker? When not caught in your addiction, have you worked hard and brought engagement and creativity to your work? When you weren't loaded, were your responsible and dependable? What ways have you done a good job for your employer or for yourself if you were self-employed?

- **My qualities** – It's easy to overlook our own positive qualities. I took up golf a couple years ago and was surprised to see how determined I was to improve, how I practiced and studied the game with such intensity. Then I realized that this quality of determination had always been there in things that I loved, like music and meditation. I'd always thought of myself as a bit lazy, but then I realized that it was only when I didn't care about something that I didn't work hard at it.

  Reflect on any qualities in yourself that might have been unacknowledged. This might mean reviewing your life to see patterns of behavior—positive patterns—that you've never recognized before.

  Here are some more positive qualities and behaviors you might consider:

- Patience
- Honesty
- Integrity
- Service
- Being a good listener
- Determination in program/practice
- Determination in your work

- Creativity
- Insightfulness
- Morality
- Intuitiveness
- Analytical

It can be helpful to make your own list of positive qualities.

Seven Factors of Enlightenment

The Seven Factors of Enlightenment are the qualities that the Buddha said we need to develop in order to overcome greed, hatred, and delusion and find freedom. These are qualities that grow naturally as we follow a spiritual path, but they can also be consciously developed through specific practices. By taking a Seven Factors inventory, we can see the aspects of the path that we need to work on as well as those that are already well-developed. In this way we can gain some direction for our practice and program as well as taking some comfort in our progress so far.

Exercise: Factors of Enlightenment Inventory

From time to time, ask yourself which of these qualities are developing well and which might need some extra attention and effort:

- **Mindfulness** – How strong is your mindfulness practice? Do you have a clear understanding of what mindfulness is? Do you practice formally on a regular basis? How much and in what areas do you apply mindfulness to your daily life? How could you deepen your mindfulness, both in meditation and in daily life?
- **Investigation** – Investigation is careful attention to the details of our experience, especially while meditating, and viewing that experience through the lens of dharma. This means, seeing impermanence, suffering, and the lack of a core identity in each

experience. It's not analysis, but rather a close looking. For instance, when investigating the breath, we can see that it's in constant flux; that no single breath is satisfying, that is, we always need to breathe again; and that the breath is not mine, is not me, and I am not the breath. This kind of investigation requires a close attention and effort in our practice. Are you meditating with this sense of exploration or simply sitting there?

- **Energy** - Many people struggle with energy in their practice—too much or not enough, as I discussed in the Five Hindrances. What is the quality of energy in your practice and in your life? Is it strong and balanced or do you find yourself lacking energy or too wound up? Balancing energy requires effort both during meditation and outside of meditation. During meditation, we need to work with posture and relaxation; in addition, it's important to try to extend your periods of meditation because the longer we sit, the more our energy gets naturally balanced. If we stop sitting because we're tired or restless, we never allow this natural balancing to unfold. Outside of meditation, as mentioned in the Hindrances, we need to be aware of stress, stimulation, and rest. Our culture tends to cause excess stress and stimulation and give us little time for sleep and relaxation.

- **Joy** – It's important to see that joy is one of the factors the Buddha says is vital for spiritual development. Are you enjoying your life? If not, it's vital to explore what is standing in the way. Of course we all have difficulties and many addicts struggle with depression and anxiety, but this doesn't mean we can't find ways to enjoy ourselves. Many books and workshops are around to help us cultivate joy. One workshop I recommend is *Awakening Joy*, by James Baraz, a Buddhist teacher. The other question is, are you enjoying your meditation? Sometimes our spiritual practice can start to seem like one long slog, bleak and serious.

Meditation can, and I daresay, should, be enjoyable, at least some of the time. If you're not enjoying it, why not?

- **Tranquility** – Obviously one of the things we are trying to get from meditation is a sense of tranquility. Do you see this arising in your practice? Again, we can't make tranquility happen, but if we are patient, it tends to come. If this is a particular issue, you might work with concentration or relaxation exercises in your practice.

- **Concentration** – Concentration is the quality of meditation that requires the most time and commitment. Silent meditation retreats are designed to allow this quality to grow. In daily practice it can be difficult to develop much quiet. Consider taking a silent retreat to begin to experience deeper states of calm and concentration. When meditating, devote a certain amount of time in each session to simply calming the mind.

- **Equanimity** – Equanimity is the quality of balance that allows us to not get too high or too low; it means we can accept whatever is arising in the body and mind. It is a state of deep peace. The Buddha treasured equanimity as the highest form of happiness, and included it in several lists, the Brahma Viharas (Divine Abodes), the Four Jhanas (Meditative Absorptions), and the Seven Factors of Enlightenment. Equanimity is a quality of non-reactivity which is vital for a person in recovery. It implies patience, forbearance, and endurance. It includes acceptance and serenity. It means we are not disturbed by the vicissitudes of life. Begin to be more aware of the things that disturb your equanimity, and also notice the times when you are at peace. Try to cultivate and incorporate the things that bring more equanimity into your life.

For all Seven Factors of Enlightenment, the key is practice. We can't expect these qualities just to appear because we want them to. We have to do the work that allows them to arise. At the same time, it's not helpful to judge or criticize ourselves because one or another—or all seven— aren't developed in the way we think they should be. In fact, my intention in listing the Factors is for you to take joy in seeing that many of these things are already present or at least accessible to you.

Step Five

"Admitted to God, to ourselves, and to another human being the exact nature of our wrongs."

What's This Step About?

Step Five is where we share the inventory, and thus includes Right Speech. Here we discover the power of self-revealing. Honest, open speech frees us from the fear and shame of secrets and lies. We start to discover the world of compassion and forgiveness as we get feedback from our sponsor or spiritual guide. By making honest communication a habitual part of our lives, we begin to live with more integrity. Speaking the truth also helps us to learn about ourselves as we are forced to confront in a coherent way the sometimes vague and ill-formed thoughts that hound us.

In the Western Buddhist world, it seems to be hard for people to honestly share their suffering. When you come into a Buddhist center it all seems so pure and spiritual that you can get the feeling that anything sordid or unpleasant shouldn't be mentioned, and you certainly don't want to tell anyone about your drinking, drugging or other unskillful behavior. The result can be a conspiracy of silence in which, like a dysfunctional family, problems are kept hidden and everyone acts as if everything is fine when it isn't.

This came home to me once again at a recent 10-day retreat I was teaching. The retreat was focused on deep concentration practices and conducted in silence. For the first week or so, people came to their interviews with me and spoke almost exclusively about their meditation and how it was going. Most people seemed to be doing well, and all their focus was on going deeper into the peace of meditation and developing insights. In the last few days of the retreat, though, people started to bring up different topics with me: this one said he had a drinking problem he wanted to discuss; that one was worried about her son's drug use; another person was dealing with his dependence on medication to manage his anxiety; another wanted to share her difficulty with a very traditional 12 Step group she belonged to. What I was seeing, once again, was that beneath the veneer of peace and love that the silence of the retreat cultivated, were all the real life problems people were dealing with. And deep meditation experiences weren't really fixing these problems.

Twelve Step groups aren't the most peaceful places in the world, and obviously I believe that a serious and committed meditation practice is a tremendous support to recovery. But addiction thrives in silence, even the silence of meditation. The main "practice" of 12 Step groups is the practice of sharing, of revealing ourselves in a safe public forum. Here we peel back the layers of denial and shame and get down to what's really real. It turns out that being honest about our addiction, about our self-hatred, about our pain and suffering is one of the most healing practices of all.

For me, opening up in meetings was the beginning of real growth in recovery. It surprised me to discover that when I shared my struggles, I felt better afterward. And hearing others reveal themselves often helped me to feel less isolated and unique. I realized that I'm not the only one with inner pain and confusion.

Exercise: Sharing Your Inventories

Referring back to what you wrote or thought about in Step Four, share your various inventories, including the Positive Inventory, with a sponsor, friend, or other trusted person.

Notice what comes up in anticipation of sharing your inventory.

During the act of sharing the inventory, forgotten incidents, experiences, and qualities may be recalled. Don't hesitate to add these to your recitation.

Right Speech

Although Step Five is formally about just sharing our inventory, I want to use it as a place to discuss the whole realm of communication. Right Speech, as we've seen, is part of the Noble Eightfold Path as well as one of the Five Precepts, so it's clearly important to our spiritual practice. How we communicate is the foundation of all our relationships, so it's a skill we need to work on.

The outline of the Buddha's instructions on Right Speech is this:

1. Speak the truth,

2. In a timely manner,

3. And only if useful and kind.

If we are able to apply these three tests to all of our speech, our lives will change radically. Of course, in my experience, it hasn't been possible to be so rigorous. Nonetheless, just understanding what this might look like and at least occasionally succeeding in my attempts to follow these guidelines has had a significant effect on my speech and my life.

To begin with, speaking the truth is challenging, not just in the sense of not lying or distorting the facts, but first in really understanding what is true, and second in seeing how I use language, often unintentionally, to distort the truth. For example, as I mentioned previously, I used to say something like, "I'm always depressed." One of my teachers called me on this, asking me if there were any times when I wasn't depressed. Of course there were, and are, so this was simply not true. What's important about this isn't so much that I was exaggerating, but that my statement was reinforcing a negative belief. As long as I believed that I was "always depressed," I had a pretty bleak view of my life and moods. Being more honest lifted some of that negativity, and as my teacher suggested, when I started to notice the times when I *wasn't* depressed, instead of focusing on the times I was, my mood actually improved because I had a more positive view of my emotions.

Of course, my way of stating this was for effect, as exaggeration usually is. But the recognition of the effects of exaggeration opened up a whole realm of speech for me. I started to notice when I was exaggerating, and thus, not speaking the truth. I saw how those exaggerations often triggered emotions or were meant to trigger emotions in others—they were used to manipulate. Thus, my lack of Right Speech was more than just a theoretical or even moral issue, but something that was tied directly to my relationships. As I began to be more scrupulous in my use of language and attempts to be honest, I found that my relationships tended to become cleaner; there was less conflict and confusion, less drama.

Exercise: Speaking the Truth

Commit yourself to speaking the truth for one week. Start to notice how you exaggerate, oversimplify, or otherwise distort the truth in your speech. Notice how you use language. Words like "Never," "Always," "Should," and "Can't." These words make categorical statements, and often we use them inaccurately. If I say, "You should stop drinking," how do I know that? I could make the same point by saying, "I think you should stop drinking." Or if I say, "I never get angry," is that really true? I might be safer saying, "I rarely get angry." When you find yourself about to make a categorical statement, see if it can be rephrased to be more accurate. "It seems as if," or "I usually," or "I feel as if," can be just enough moderation to be making an accurate statement. Sometimes the words will spill out, but if you notice what you've said, you can backtrack and rephrase.

* * *

Speaking in a timely manner is another interesting issue. Sometimes we get a clear sense that someone really needs some help or guidance and blurt it out when the person's not ready to hear it. For instance, telling someone that they have a drinking or drug problem when things are going okay for them, or worse, when they're high, will almost inevitably get a negative reaction. Picking the right moment takes care and sensitivity.

Exercise: Speaking in a Timely Manner

The next time you have something serious to tell someone, notice if it's the right time. You might find you already have an instinct for this; most of us do. The key is to remember to follow your instinct. Does the person seem open at this time? Do you feel balanced enough to speak in a non-judgmental manner? Are the circumstances right? For instance, are you somewhere that you won't be interrupted? Is there plenty of time to talk? Do you both have energy right now?

It's vital that we pick our moments for important conversations. Sometimes it's better to put off saying something if the situation isn't conducive to honest, open dialog.

* * *

Speaking what is useful and kind presents another challenge. How do we know if it's useful? Does "kind" always mean saying something nice? This instruction requires that we become more sensitive and mindful of others and ourselves.

Most of us have learned that telling someone the truth—at least, the truth as you see it—isn't always helpful. Of course, there's the obvious case of being asked how you like someone's new outfit. But there are much more serious situations when it's not helpful to tell someone the truth. This doesn't mean we lie, but more that we avoid speaking at all. Saying nothing can be one of the most skillful uses of speech in many situations. This is called "restraint of tongue and pen," and also applies to electronic communication.

Many times I've received or heard others give advice that was either not timely or delivered in such a way as to be offputting. In 12 Step programs there are lots of helpful suggestions, but all-too-often these suggestions are delivered without thought about how ready our audience is to hear our advice. When we tell a newcomer "You have to find a Higher Power," or "You shouldn't get in a relationship in your first year," we may be giving time-tested advice, but the newcomer may not be ready to get this advice. Maybe the person is an atheist, or perhaps he or she is feeling very lonely and the thought of going a year alone is too much to bear right now.

Exercise: Useful and Kind

The admonition to speak what is useful and kind can come into conflict with the guidance that we speak the truth. It may be true that someone is overweight, but telling them so might not be kind. It might be kind to tell someone they are doing a good job at work, but it might not be true. At these times we often find that silence is the best thing. Of course, that's not always an option, and in fact, we sometimes find that what's most useful and kind doesn't actually make the person feel better at this moment. Telling an addict that she needs to get clean may not be the nicest thing, but ultimately it may be the kindest. So, being kind doesn't always mean we're trying to make people feel good—at least in the short term--but rather that we want to help.

* * *

By now you can probably see that the combination of these three admonitions, to speak the truth in a timely manner if it is useful and kind is quite a challenge. Just to accomplish one of these is difficult enough, but to do them all at once is really tough. In the Twelve Step tradition we have a saying: "Progress not perfection." This applies. The development of more skillful ways of speaking is an ongoing process, much like learning meditation, or simply trying to be a better person. We start out just by bringing more attention to how we talk to people, being more mindful. Whatever we discover is our starting point. We investigate whether we are fulfilling the elements of Right Speech. Then we can start to bring more intention to our communication.

Of course, not all communication is equally important or sensitive. What we really want to do is learn to handle the more delicate moments and the moments of high emotionality more skillfully. Sometimes we'll actually know these moments are coming as with some appointment or plan we have to talk with someone. We can think ahead about what we want to say and how we want to say it, reviewing the Right Speech guidelines. Other times, of course, situations will arise where we have no chance to prepare. We might find ourselves in the middle of an argument or testy exchange when we suddenly remember the guidelines. Even then it's not too late. We can take a breath and back off a bit.

Even if we only remember the guidelines *after* an unskillful exchange it's better than nothing. Little by little we train ourselves, even if only in retrospect. The important thing is to keep the guidelines in mind as much as possible, to keep our intention to speak skillfully, and over time we'll discover that change has happened.

Self Revealing, Compassion, and Forgiveness

Ajahn Amaro likes to quote a survey that once found a majority of people are more afraid of public speaking than of dying. His conclusion: "People are more afraid of ego death than physical death." To speak about our addiction and our foolish, destructive, and humiliating behavior can be even more frightening than the usual public speech or professional presentation. Nonetheless, that's what Twelve Step meetings often involve. What most of us discover, though, is that such openness and confession is not humiliating but freeing. And once it becomes a regular thing, we start to depend on the healing power of self-revealing.

Many of us, and certainly this is true of addicts, walk around feeling alone with our thoughts and feelings. Naturally enough people don't open up about their inner struggles to many people. A lifetime of addiction, self-hatred, and all the unskillful acts we commit builds up quite an inventory of shame, and this pain can sustain our addiction, or if we are clean and sober, it can keep us from finding any real peace in our program.

Learning to reveal ourselves is like any other habit. At first it feels awkward and unnatural, but over time it becomes natural. Of course, I'm talking about 12 Step programs or some other equally safe place to share this intimate information. In that kind of setting, the community holds our words with understanding and acceptance—and confidentiality. We are speaking to people who understand, who have been there. What we quickly learn is that we are not really alone, that what we think, feel, say, and do is common to all humans. In silence our flaws seem uniquely shameful. When we learn that they aren't unique, the shame goes out of them. This is a critical discovery on a recovery path and on a spiritual journey because this insight opens us to compassion and true forgiveness.

The discovery that our failings are shared by many others allows us to begin to forgive ourselves. If, rather than being uniquely flawed, we simply share common human (or at least human addict) failings, then these failings aren't our fault. They simply result from the difficulty of being a human. We all act unskillfully at times. We all hurt others. And when we're lost in our addiction—a place we didn't really choose to be—we do more hurting than usual. Coming out of this behavior, admitting our failings and trying to move on is cause for forgiveness.

On top of this, seeing how painful it was for us to live with this self-hatred, we begin to see that others share this pain, and we naturally start to feel compassion and forgiveness for them as well.

Coming out of the self-centeredness of addiction into a more open connection with others allows us to recognize these universal connections, the shared suffering of living beings.

And it all starts with self-revealing. For most of us, this first means listening to others reveal themselves. When I first got sober and started going to meetings, I was amazed by what people would say, how honest they could be about their thoughts, feelings, and behavior. What struck me, too, was the laughter in the meetings as someone told their, sometimes horrifying, story and deepest secrets. We laugh because we understand, because we've been there. It took some time before I was willing to go to the same level of honesty, but when I did, that's when my recovery really began.

Up till that point, I was still holding back from really being a part of the 12 Step community. I'd never been a joiner, and so I figured if I just went to meetings and listened I'd get what I needed. But a year into my sobriety, I found that being an observer simply wasn't enough. Yes, I was staying sober, but things weren't really changing in my life. I still was expecting a relationship to fix me, and I realized that the loneliness I was trying to purge might be healed better by a 12 Step group than another lover.

Finally I went to a small meeting and raised my hand. I shared about what I was going through, and immediately the group seemed to pick me up and hold me. After the meeting people talked to me and supported me. It felt completely different from the effect of standing in the back of meetings and listening. Now I was right in the middle of the action and now the program began to work.

Almost immediately I made sharing at meetings a regular thing. Each time I did I felt another weight being lifted. Some years

BARNES&NOBLE

www.bn.com

Ship To:
Maria Falchier
9 West South Orange Ave.
Apt. 214
South Orange, NJ 07079
USA

Customer Service:
1-800-THE-BOOK
http://help.barnesandnoble.com

PO Num: 0026187114

Loc: PM0103
Box Size: TFT5

e Ave.

7079

ay 03, 2016 **(Order No. 4014705302 / BM 4014705302)**

	Item #	Item Price	Total
and the Twelve Steps: A Recovery for Individual	9780615942216	13.63	13.63

Pay Method: VISA   **Credit Card#:** 1274

From:
Maria Falchier
9 West South Orange Ave.
Apt. 214
South Orange, NJ 07079
USA

To:
Barnes & Noble.com
B&N.COM Customer Returns
1 Barnes & Noble Way
Monroe Township, NJ 08831
USA

(401)4705302

THANK YOU FOR YOUR ORDER!

9905000000111 0199614

05/05/2016 12:00 AM   (EAD)

05/04/2016 5:28 PM   (PRINT)

Your order of N

Qty	Descripti
1	**Buddhis**
	Workbo

Our readiness, the strength of our intention, must be there before any significant change happens. The Buddha was very clear: no action occurs without intention.

Joseph Goldstein tells a story of his early time in India. One day he went for a long walk, and on the way back he decided to test this idea. He stopped walking and tried to see if he could start again without the intention to walk. For long minutes he stood still watching his intention. Nothing happened.

Of course, most of the time we walk around and don't notice the intention behind it. But if we start to pay close attention we'll see that it's always there, behind every action. And this is the point, that we need to pay close attention to our intention if we want to make wise choices in our lives. If we don't take care with intention, our habitual pleasure-seeking and ego-striving will dominate our actions. Those impulses are strong and can only be uprooted with effort. We must see them and not act on them.

This is what Step Six is ultimately about, cultivating Right Intention.

Getting Ready

How then do we get ready to change? How do we cultivate Right Intention?

In some sense, this is a Catch 22. Right Intention seems to come forth from the desire to change; and the desire to change seems to come out of Right Intention. But what seems to be the fundamental trigger for many of us to start to deal with the issues in our lives is the recognition of our own suffering. When we see clearly the pain in our lives, the pain that we are creating through our own actions or inaction, we become motivated.

Denial of our problems is a kind of willful turning away from the truth. To be inspired to change, we need to turn toward the truth. Denial is not just an intellectual or emotional avoidance, but can manifest in our addiction as we try to avoid pain and problems by using. As long as we are avoiding the truth by whatever means, we will be able to forestall change.

By this logic, then, we've arrived back at mindfulness, the need to see reality clearly, to feel our pain and let that pain act as a motivator. But it seems to me that engaging in mindfulness also requires a readiness to change, or at least a readiness to look closely at what's going on in our heart-mind.

All of this points to the difficulty in arousing motivation when it's not spontaneous. Oftentimes it seems that the people who are able to get into recovery and begin a meaningful process of change gracefully do it by luck or magic or some innate capacity—in other words, not through a process of cause and effect that can be identified. This is one of the reasons that people sometimes attribute their recovery or their spiritual transformation to God. I don't accept this answer, and I actually think it's not just magical thinking, but a lazy explanation. It's easier to write something off as the hand of God than it is to look deeply into the process. But I believe that coming to understand, at least to some extent, how we grow and change is a valuable and important exploration that gives us vital information in life's ongoing struggles. If we are always depending on some undefinable, uncontrollable force we call "God," we are abdicating responsibility, and worse, making ourselves vulnerable to relapse and other dangers. Our only protection is our faith, and faith is notoriously fickle when things go wrong.

This is why I encourage people to explore the process of their recovery as I did I in Step Two's exercise, "Tracing back Recovery." Here is another exercise along those lines.

Exercise: How Do I Change?

Take some time to deconstruct one or more of the ways you have changed in your life. This can be done as a written exercise if you find that useful.

Go back to the earliest point you can remember that you realized you needed to do something. Go through the process, including actions you took, emotional triggers, and information that helped you.
Ask yourself these three questions:

- What **gets in the way** of change and letting go for me?
- What **helps me** to change and let go?
- How can I **cultivate those qualities** that help me to change and let go?

Exercise: Raising Our Bottom

One of the main things that makes us willing to change is seeing our suffering. Isn't this why we stopped drinking and using in the first place? Start to use your mindfulness practice to become more sensitive to how you create suffering in your life.
Notice the things you cling to that cause suffering:

- Notice the thoughts that cause suffering, the judgments and opinions.
- Notice the activities that cause suffering.
- Notice the ways your addiction still manifests in unskillful craving.

What Will I Lose?

One of the great challenges of Step Six is facing the fear of losing our identity. In some ways we may feel that our "character defects" define us. Although, by the time I got to Step Six I'd given up the belief that drinking and using was cool, I still liked to think of myself as hip. I was a musician; I'd lived an alternative lifestyle; and I looked down on people who had conventional jobs and followed a conventional path in life. Getting sober in LA even let me rub shoulders occasionally with rock stars and movie celebrities, to some extent, further feeding my view of myself as special.

At a year sober, still harboring dreams of a successful musical career, I got the opportunity to work as an intern for a record company. My fantasy was that I'd become a record producer, now that my own performing career was winding down. But that's not exactly how things played out.

As the assistant to one of the executives I was asked to do a certain amount of typing on a computer. Never having typed and never having operated a computer (this was the mid-1980's) I pecked away and did my best. After a year at the company with no paying job opening up, I realized it was a dead end. But I'd learned one thing: typing and operating a computer were job skills that might help me. So I enrolled in an adult education course in my neighborhood, took typing and an introduction to computers. A couple months later, armed with my new skills, I applied for a job at Santa Monica School District. Soon I found myself getting up every morning, putting on khakis and a buttoned-down shirt, and going in to work in their personnel department.

It was an odd experience for me, living this normal life, having health benefits and getting a paycheck every other week. It represented everything I thought I didn't want in my life, but the funny thing was I liked it. I'd spent many years worrying about money, working with unreliable musicians and shady bar owners, and now I started to understand why people chose to live a more conventional life.

At the same time, though, it felt as if I was living someone else's life, like I'd slipped into another person's skin. Who was this guy who sat at a desk typing and answering phones? Showing up on time? Being polite and helpful? Had I lost something or gained something? Had I become a different person?

Looking back, it's pretty clear that what I'd lost was mostly about ego and self-image. That self-image hadn't made me happy, and the lifestyle that image demanded wasn't very enjoyable. Would I change that if I could? No, because I'd had the opportunity to be a musician, to follow my passion, and to take risks that many people wouldn't have done. But the time had come to change—I could say, "to grow up," but that seems demeaning of who I'd been. The growing up wasn't really about giving up music, but about the greater question of addiction and irresponsibility, of which my work life was just one aspect. Nonetheless, here I was in a new skin—and new clothes—and there was an adjustment. What became clear, though, is that what was actually happening was that I was becoming more free.

As a musician I'd thought that I'd had great freedom. I didn't have to show up at an office nine-to-five; I didn't have a boss; I didn't have to follow the rules of conventional society. But what I now realized was that my musical career had been a prison of my own making. That's because I didn't believe that I had any options. Initially when I decided to be a musician it felt like a choice. But over time, I came to believe that not only was music the only thing I *wanted* to do, but that it was the only thing I was *capable* of. This attitude had developed out of my high school experience as I became depressed and lost interest and motivation in school, and then got worse when I went into the work world with no skills or education, finding myself suited only for the most menial of jobs. Left with music, which of course was my love, I was anything but free, instead a victim of my own fears, aversions, and prejudices.

Now, working at the school district, a world of possibilities started to open up. The realization that my thinking had been terribly distorted motivated me to start questioning all kinds of things, my attitudes about school, about relationships, about politics, and more. I became engaged in life in a way I hadn't been since I'd been a kid. My world started to open up. I had become "entirely ready" to, not only let go, but to embrace my new life.

Exercise: What Am I Afraid to Lose?

Take some contemplative time to ask yourself about your worldview and self-image. Then, write down the things you are afraid of losing.

- Are there qualities you have that you think make you special? Are these serving you?
- What attitudes do you have that might be destructive regarding yourself; your lifestyle; your relationships; your worklife; society, culture, and politics?
- What would happen if you dropped your self-beliefs? What different choices might you make in your life?

The Problems of Language

Throughout the 12 Steps there are potential pitfalls in the language, and Step Six has a few. I've discussed the word "God" in other places, so I won't address that again here. But the word "defects" is one that people often rebel against, especially when tied to "character." To suggest that we are defective, like something that needs to be returned to the factory, is a pretty harsh way of describing someone. And character is something that seems innate, something solid and unchangeable. With this view it's easy to understand why one would think that they needed the intervention of a supreme being to undo their problems. Normal efforts wouldn't seem to be enough to undo a defective character. Only God could handle that job.

From a Buddhist viewpoint, though, character as a permanent, solid set of traits makes no sense. Nothing is solid; nothing is permanent. Everything is mutable; everything is in flux. Yes, we may have tendencies and personality traits, but most of these can have positive *or* negative manifestations, that is, the traits themselves aren't necessarily bad, but how we express them is more important. For instance, if a person is generous, that sounds good, but if they give away so much that they can't take care of themselves, it's harmful. I used to think that my tendency to fantasize was a negative trait until I realized that my creativity as a musician and writer arose from the same aspect. Rather than "character defects," I would talk about "unskillful thoughts, words, and actions." This puts less of a judgmental spin on things and points to the fact that the problem lies not with a blanket issue, but with the individual moments in our lives and how we are behaving.

Exercise: Finding Your Own Language

Reflect on the words you find difficult in the 12 Steps, and see if there are alternatives that work better for you.

Here are a few of the typical trigger words:

- Powerless
- God
- Defects of character
- Moral inventory
- Shortcomings

Defects and Buddha Nature

The term "defects of character" is one that many people find disturbing. Character seems like something essential, something that defines us, and if mine is defective, it doesn't make me feel very good about myself. Of course, from the standpoint of impermanence and not-self, none of our personal qualities are fixed, but nonetheless, it's easy to fall into a negative belief about thoughts, feelings, and behaviors that are persistent in our lives.

The other extreme is to see everything we do as our "Buddha Nature," that we're already enlightened, perfect, and should let go of all judgments. This is a distortion of the idea of Buddha Nature, which is that beneath the Five Hindrances, when the mind is cleared of distractions and delusions, there is a purity. This is certainly true, but that purity is not a personal quality, simply the natural purity of awareness. If we take this personally, claiming that it belongs to us or is something special about us, we are corrupting the very meaning of Buddha Nature.

These two extremes, one of seeing ourselves as defective and the other as seeing ourselves as perfect, don't allow growth or healing. If our character is defective, well, that's just the way it is, we'll never change; if we're already perfect, then we can go on acting the way we are, safely justified in our behaviors.

Each of these views is dangerous because how we see ourselves has profound influence on our behavior and our feelings. If we feel that we our character is defective there can be a sense of despair or resignation that both leaves us unhappy and paralyzed. We feel bad about who we are, guilty, ashamed, downtrodden, and because we see these qualities as inherent to who we are, we don't see any possibility of change. The belief that we can't change is a self-fulfilling prophecy: if I believe I can't change, then I won't try to change, and thus, I won't change.

The other extreme, that I'm already perfect, that my behavior is always just Buddha Nature expressing itself creates another kind of paralysis. In this case, since nothing's wrong, there's no need to change or grow. This is a particularly pernicious delusion that allows for all kinds of unskillful behavior, from addiction to promiscuity to abuse and arrogance. No matter how we feel, how we behave, or what happens in our life, we can file it all under "natural unfolding" and reject any sense of responsibility or need to deal with the consequences of our actions. Of course, this kind of behavior eventually catches up with us, with results that are often disastrous for us and for others. When this arrogance infects a spiritual leader, it can destroy an entire community.

The Buddha's Middle Way suggests another viewpoint: we aren't inherently flawed, but we still have some work to do. In fact, the idea of impermanence and a fluid identity gives us hope that we can really change. As in Step Two, this view acknowledges that the

Law of Karma, that all actions have results, implies the possibility of growth and change. There is neither a fixed condition—our defects—nor a magical spiritual state that is immutable. Our "character" is dependent upon our actions; our spiritual condition is a direct result of the work we do on ourselves and the ways we express ourselves in the world.

Exercise: Understanding Our Inventory

Take some time to reflect on the negative qualities that appeared in your Fourth Step inventory. If it's helpful, write them down as a list. Once you've got an idea of what these qualities are here are some things to do with the list:

- Ask yourself what strategies might be most helpful in countering or letting go of these qualities. These strategies will be the basis for the work of Step Seven.

- Think of times when you *weren't* acting on these "defects." For instance, if one defect is selfishness, remember a time when you acted kindly or generously. Go through all the negative qualities in this way. See that you aren't always a bad person.

- Ask yourself if all these negative qualities are here right now. Probably not. If they aren't here now then how can they be permanent flaws?

- Recognize that each of these qualities is a *human* quality, not yours personally. You are by no means the only person to have this quality. These are shared by most of the human race, especially the addicts.

- Ask yourself if these qualities have changed over time, particularly since you've been working a program. Most of us see that as we work the Steps and deepen our spiritual life, our negative qualities not only weaken, but sometimes transmute into something positive.

Step Seven

"Humbly asked Him to remove our shortcomings."

What's This Step About?

Step Seven is about letting go. Clearly that's what the Buddhist path is about as well, letting go of the cause of suffering. When detached from the idea of some Supreme Being fixing us, this Step draws one of the most direct lines between the 12 Steps and Buddhism. To make this connection, though, I think we need to understand the language of the Step in a different way.

Ajahn Buddhadasa says that when we pray we are "beseeching the Law of Karma through our actions, not merely with words," and this I think encapsulates the Buddhist approach to this Step. We aren't just saying some words to ask God to remove our shortcomings, we are actively engaging in a process that goes against our longterm, conditioned thoughts, words, and deeds to bring change in our lives. By living in a new way, our life is renewed; by addressing our destructive habits and ceasing to act on those impulses we are breaking down the power of addiction; by taking up new behaviors and attitudes we are creating new karmic patterns that bear fruit in every aspect of our lives. "Letting go" isn't really a passive activity. When we let go of our drinking, drugging, binging, or other addiction, it's an intensely engaged, challenging, and energetic act. It takes a lot of counter-action to get into recovery—actions that go against our historical behaviors.

Step Seven may be the crux of the whole recovery process. It's right there in the numerical middle of the Steps; it springs from the two most powerful elements of the Step process, our relationship with a Higher Power and our inventory work; it embodies what recovery is all about, letting go; and it requires us to "keep coming back" to the Step because for most of us, our shortcomings are persistent and ever-evolving, requiring a lifetime commitment to the work of letting go.

Exercise: Beseeching the Law of Karma

Looking at your inventory and the habitual patterns that were revealed in that exploration, make a commitment to take the actions that will bring change to these habits. Look at some of the strategies that you listed in Step Six. Consider employing some of these tools for change:

- Meditation
- Commitment to Precepts
- 12 Step (or other recovery community) participation
- Therapy
- Health and wellness, especially movement, exercise and diet

Antidotes to the Five Hindrances

From the standpoint of Buddhism, what we need to let go of, what causes suffering, is the Five Hindrances, desire, aversion, sleepiness, restlessness, and doubt. While we've explored these in Step Four, now, as we begin the process of change and "removing our defects of character" we can look at some of the ways to work with these challenging qualities.

We could say there are two approaches to working with the hindrances: mindfulness and abandoning. They can, in fact, work together. First we see them clearly, then we takes steps to get rid of them or transcend them.

The mindful approach means that we are trying to fully engage the hindrance. Mostly we don't see the hindrances clearly because we are just reacting to them. So, when we stop and say, "what does this feel like?" and explore the energy in the body and the mood tone, then we stop running from them and start actually experiencing them.

With desire and aversion, perhaps what's most important is to see how they cause us suffering. When we look closely, whether during meditation or just in our daily lives, we will see how this gnawing craving and aversion create an underlying discomfort in our lives. Seeing this discomfort is sometimes enough to inspire us to let go. This might mean, simply coming back to the breath in meditation, or it might mean making some real changes in our lives, in our work, our relationships, or anything that tends to consume us.

The classical antidote to desire is seeing the impermanent, insubstantial, and unsatisfying nature of that which we desire. This can involve contemplation around pleasure or ownership, or anything we are wanting. The vacation we are dreaming about will end and we will be back at work; the new car we can't wait for will age, get scratched, and wear out; our relationship with the person we so desire will inevitably change, and will have struggles and cool off.

The classical antidote to aversion is developing lovingkindness (metta) and compassion (karuna). When we see that all beings strive for happiness, and all beings are subject to sickness, old age, death, and loss, we realize that even the person we hate hungers for the same things we do. When people harm us it is out of their own pain and confusion, and is also going to cause them pain at some time in the future, so we try to feel compassion for them. The practices of Metta and Karuna help us develop these qualities.

The classical antidotes to sleepiness include sitting straighter, breathing deeply, opening the eyes, and finally, standing up. It's also recommended that we see if we are eating too much, as that also causes drowsiness.

The classical antidote to restlessness is to do a concentration practice like counting the breaths or repeating a mantra. In practice, this can be difficult. I suggest trying to practice with a sense of a more "spacious" mind that doesn't feel so trapped by restlessness. The "Opening to Space" meditation in Step Eleven can help with this.

Doubt takes two forms: doubt of the teachings or teachers and doubt of ourselves. The classical antidote to doubt of the teachings is to study and practice. The best way to develop trust in the practice is to sit. Over time practice almost invariably deepens, and that deepening gives us more confidence in the path. In addition, when we read or sit with wise teachers, we come to understand the Dharma more clearly, and this also supports our faith.

As for doubt in ourselves, this is more challenging and is probably best dealt with through some of the "Cognitive Inventory" practices offered in Step Ten. We need to see through our own self-doubt, to see that it is unsubstantiated, to break our negative beliefs.

In his brilliant book *Satipatthana: The Direct Path to Realization*, Analayo gives some more antidotes, and one that appears for every single hindrance is "good friends and suitable conversation." For those in a 12 Step program, this isn't surprising.

We know how helpful and supportive it can be to have spiritual friends and how they help us to get out of our selves, to break our inner dialog and negative thinking. In community, in meetings, or in sangha we find respite from self-centeredness, and we hear words of wisdom that remind us of our higher intentions.

Exercise: Antidotes to the Hindrances in Meditation

During your next sitting, explore what hindrances are arising. When you notice a hindrance, first just try to be open and mindful of what you are experiencing. Then try applying these antidotes to the hindrances:

- Desire – notice its unsatisfactory quality, the tension or feeling of grasping in the body. Notice the impermanent and unsatisfactory quality of that which we desire.
- Aversion – notice its unsatisfactory quality, the unpleasant physical experience. Offer lovingkindness and compassion to the people and things you resist and resent.
- Sleepiness – sit up straighter; take some deeper breaths; open the eyes. Investigate the experience more closely.
- Restlessness – First try one of the concentration practices found in Step Eleven. If this doesn't work, consciously relax, release tension on an outbreath, and work with a sense of spaciousness.
- Doubt – notice the judgmental quality of doubt, its basis in conditioned, unsubstantiated views. Study the dharma and practice more extensively.

Experiment with these antidotes, and also explore creatively your own ways of dealing with the hindrances.

The Three Elements of Samadhi

The Buddha's Noble Eightfold Path is sometimes divided into three categories, Sila, Samadhi, and Panna, or Morality, Meditation, and

Wisdom. The three aspects of the Eightfold Path that fall under Samadhi are Right Effort, Right Mindfulness, and Right Concentration. It is these that we cultivate and utilize in our formal meditation practice. Many of the books written on Buddhist meditation are essentially addressing these three elements, so there is a great deal that can be said about them. I'd like to see if we could look at them as a set of synergistic tools.

Here's one way of encapsulating meditation: we need to relax, while staying alert; pay close attention to our moment-to-moment experience without judgment, grasping, or resistance; and we need to sustain our attention long enough to become deeply settled in the present moment. Blending relaxation and alertness is the realm of Right Effort; paying attention without judgment is the realm of Right Mindfulness; sustaining the attention and effort is the realm of Right Concentration. So we can see that these three aspects of meditation aren't separate and in fact won't create real change without interacting.

Nonetheless, these elements are often viewed separately. Often I'm asked how to stay awake during meditation, how to deal with pain in the body, or how to stop thoughts from disturbing meditation. These are questions of effort. But they can't be separated from questions of mindfulness and concentration because in order to deal with sleepiness, pain, or thoughts, we need to be mindful and we need to sustain that mindfulness.

At other times, I hear it suggested that mindfulness is just about a passive acceptance of whatever is arising in our mind or body. While I can see that acceptance is a vital aspect of meditation, it's not always skillful to just "let it be." Sometimes we need to act or arouse engaged activity, to respond to what we see with wisdom.

Finally, many meditators seek out the pleasure and peace of concentration with no particular interest in the insights that come with mindfulness. Some people have the capacity to get quite calm and even blissed-out while sitting in meditation. However, such altered states have no great benefit beyond the few moments of calm they provide. Without mindfulness and an engaged effort, concentration can, in fact, be used like a drug, as an escape from life, rather than an opening into life.

We can see, then, that developing Right Effort, Right Mindfulness, and Right Concentration together is the most effective way to learn meditation and to derive the most benefit from a meditation practice.

Meditation: Blending Effort, Mindfulness, and Concentration

Each of these elements is addressed in exercises in other parts of this book, but here I'd like to talk more about their interaction.

Blending effort, mindfulness, and concentration takes an engaged attitude. As we sit in meditation, we need to ask ourselves what is needed in this moment, more effort or less effort? More mindfulness? More concentration? What is the quality of my effort right now? Easeful or grasping? Lazy or alert? Am I being truly mindful of the breath or just drifting along? Am I giving myself enough time and stillness to allow concentration to develop or is my restlessness undermining peace?

It's this kind of questioning and observing that we need during meditation. Ironically, this seemingly passive activity really needs a lot of energy. Somehow, we have to discover the "zone" where we are awake and relaxed without getting restless, sleepy, or spaced out. This isn't easy, and for most people, it doesn't happen overnight. It comes as a result of persistent, regular, and sustained practice.

Meditation: Aspects of Effort

Refining and balancing effort is at the heart of meditation practice. The great challenge of this balancing is the paradox of striving: if we are grasping at a result in our meditation we are, by definition, causing our own suffering, but if we aren't making any effort, nothing changes.

As you look at your own effort in meditation, here are three elements to explore:

Sitting still: Physical stillness is part of meditation. Maintaining stillness helps the development of concentration and it allows a clearer mindfulness. Some teachers challenge their students to take a vow to sit absolutely still for certain meditation periods. For most of us, sitting still for periods from twenty minutes to as long as an hour or more is challenging. Especially if you are in a lotus posture of any kind, you are likely to experience discomfort sitting still. And then there are things like the urge to scratch an itch or restlessness that make you want to shift your posture. If we give in to every urge to move, we'll discover that the mind tends to move with the body, and we'll have a hard time getting settled. Nonetheless, there are times when the knees hurt so much or we are simply consumed with a desire to change posture, when resisting movement is actually causing more agitation than the movement would if we succumbed to the urge. In these moments, it can be wise to simply shift the attention to the desire, and then pay close, mindful attention to the experience of moving. Then, return to stillness.

I will explore the challenges of working with physical pain later in the book.

Thoughts: Working with thoughts is one of the most challenging aspects of meditation. Many beginners have the impression that they are supposed to stop thinking all together, and believe that they are meditating poorly or wrong if thoughts are still in the mind during their meditation. This reflects a basic misunderstanding of meditation.

Thoughts are somewhat inevitable in meditation. As human beings, our power of thought is our primary means of survival, what sets us apart from all the other beings on the planet. To think that we can just stop thinking after decades of practice and, indeed, eons of evolution, is unrealistic. And the point of mindfulness meditation isn't to just stop thoughts, anyway. Certainly it helps to get a bit more space in the mind, to not be caught up in consuming and obsessive streams of thought while meditating, but what's most important isn't to stop thoughts, but to change our relationship to thoughts.

What this means is that we start to become aware of thoughts as they appear in the mind; we start to realize when we are having selfish or destructive thoughts versus generous and helpful ones; we begin to notice the thoughts that trigger negative emotions; we recognize irrational thinking; and we get a feel for our own intuitive thoughts and wisdom. None of this is about silencing the mind, but rather strengthening the observing quality—mindfulness—and not automatically believing everything that appears in our thoughts.

We can say that we are "powerless over our thoughts," but, as with our addiction, this doesn't mean we have to continue to be driven by them. While we can stop altogether our drinking or drugging, our relationship to thoughts might be more akin to someone with an eating disorder who still has to eat everyday, but needs to approach food in a different way. We still have to think—where would we be if we didn't?— but we have to stop letting conditioned, compulsive, or automatic thoughts run our lives.

Investigation: At the heart of mindfulness and Insight Meditation is the quality of investigation. This is known as one of the Seven Factors of Enlightenment I discussed in Step Four. Investigation is the quality of closely examining our moment-to-moment experience. It isn't thinking about our experience or analyzing it, but trying to be very sensitive to what it feels like in our senses and what it is revealing to us.

The Foundations of Mindfulness point to how to approach investigation. First, we pay attention to the body and all our sense experiences; then we pay attention to impermanence of all that we observe in this way. Next we pay attention to feelings (pleasant, unpleasant, and neutral); then we pay attention to impermanence of feelings. Third, we pay attention to mind states; then we pay attention to impermanence of all that we observe in mind states. Finally, we pay attention to *dhammas* (categories of experience); then we pay attention to impermanence of all *dhammas*.

This kind of instruction can be a bit esoteric, especially when we start out in meditation. This is why introductory meditation instruction usually sticks with following the breath—an aspect of the First Foundation of Mindfulness. Nonetheless, simply working with this single focus can be an opportunity for investigation. What does the breath feel like? What does awareness of breath do to my mind and emotions? To my body? Why can't my attention stay with this one experience? What is pulling me away from the breath?

Once we've become at least passingly familiar with following the breath, we can begin to investigate thoughts. This is a critical part of mindfulness meditation, and while it needs to be done carefully so as not to become a kind of ruminative self-therapy, with a bit of instruction, it can soon bear fruit. Many people find that just beginning to notice what thoughts are passing through the mind brings insight. We are often surprised by how much time we spend on certain topics. Perhaps you realize that your work takes up inordinate amounts of space in your mind; maybe you notice that you worry about minor details of life that needn't concern you so much; or you might realize that you are carrying an underlying resentment or grief or other subconscious emotion you weren't aware of. Any of these insights, and many others, can be revealing, and ultimately freeing. As we start to observe the minor and major obsessions of our mind; the way our body reacts with stress and pain; the repetitive nature of our thoughts; and the themes that reveal the very unfolding of our lives, giants revelations can occur. Tectonic shifts take place in our lives as we begin to make conscious choices about beliefs and impulses that have unconsciously driven our lives. This is the power of investigation.

Finally, it's worth noting that investigation has one other very practical effect: it keeps us awake. As Fritz Perls, the founder of Gestalt Therapy, famously said: "Boredom is the lack of attention." In other words, everything is inherently interesting, if we just investigate. When we investigate, we become engaged and energized. So, investigation is an antidote, not just to boredom, but to the hindrance of Sloth and Torpor.

Exercise: Beseeching the Law of Karma

When Ajahn Buddhadasa said that "asking God" was the same as "beseeching the Law of Karma through our actions, not merely with words," he gave Buddhists a perfect way to understand Step Seven. While this Step has a Biblical tone to its language, when viewed as a process of karma, that is, cause and effect, it can simply be seen as taking the actions that will bring about change. The 12 Steps are often called "a program of action," so this approach fits well.

When we say "action" in this sense, we are talking about three things: thoughts, words, and deeds, because it's these three forms of action—internal and external—that create our karma. Once again, then, this Step and this exercise, are about watching our minds, our speech, and the things we do. It's only through acting in new ways, non-addictive ways, non-destructive ways, that our habits will change. We need to change our thinking, letting go of self-hatred, resentment, blaming, and despair; we need to change our speech, being honest, kind, and authentic; we need to change our actions, becoming less selfish, acting wisely, and with integrity. More than anything, it is these new ways of acting that will change us, inside and out.

We need to remember, too, that "our own best thinking" got us into this mess. We should remain open to, and indeed, actively seek, guidance from others we trust. This is, of course, the basis of the 12 Step community and another argument for participating in that fellowship.

Effort and the Dharma of Pain

Every time I teach an introductory class (and often in more advanced groups) people ask about how to work with pain in their practice. There is often an attitude that, "If I could just get my knees to stop hurting, *then* I could really meditate." I point out that, although the Buddha listed five hindrances to meditation, pain wasn't one of them.

Many of the core practices in Buddhist meditation use the body as their focus. The Buddha encouraged us to explore physical sensations in a variety of ways, and he also suggested that we should develop a mind that isn't distracted or disturbed by unpleasant sensations.

When I first started to practice, over thirty years ago, my teachers seemed more willing to push their students to work with pain than teachers do today. Part of this change has been a skillful way to help people avoid creating struggles and striving in their practice. But what has been lost, it seems, is the power of mind and heart that are developed when working directly with unpleasant sensations. My own practice has been deepened tremendously by this work, and, while it hasn't been easy, I don't see a " easier, softer" way to live in my body than to learn to be present with the range of sensory experience. In fact, learning to meditate with pain has been a great gift and inspiration in my practice, and I hope to be able to share that gift and inspiration with you.

Meeting Your Body

Moving away from pain is one of the two things that drive us toward addiction. (The other is moving towards pleasure.) Many of us used drugs, alcohol, and other substances to mask the emotional pain in our lives. Others, struggling with physical pain, became addicted to medicines that were supposed to help us. Coming into recovery doesn't mean that we stop feeling pain, but that we change our relationship to pain.

Pain is inevitable. The Buddha's First Noble Truth, the Truth of Suffering, makes this clear. The Buddha talks about all the things that are difficult and painful in life, all the way from the pain of birth to the pain of death—and lots in between. He tells us that we need to understand this truth, and by this I think he means that we need to directly face the difficulties of life, not try to avoid them. Step One of the Twelve Steps is, I think, saying the same thing: we have to admit our powerlessness, our addiction, the pain and struggle we are living in.

When people come to meditation they often see it as a way out of pain. And, certainly, there are ways that meditation can be used skillfully to relieve pain. But it's not the same as taking a pill. It's a process, one that requires commitment, compassion, and understanding.

When I first started to practice Buddhist meditation I wanted to sit like the Buddha, on the floor with my legs crossed. In those days, the early '80's, I rarely saw a chair in a meditation hall. I guess we were more infatuated with the Eastern forms, and we were younger (and more flexible)—it was rare to see someone over forty in a Buddhist center.

The first Buddhist meditation class I took was at the International Buddhist Meditation Center in Los Angeles. The meditation hall was dimly lit, with Zen calligraphy and Tibetan tankhas on the walls. Just a few of us took that weekly class, sitting on a raised part of the floor in front of the great Buddha statue. The cushions were *zafus*, the hard, round Japanese meditation pillows, and the floor was covered in a thin, bamboo mat. The teacher, an American monk just back from six years in Sri Lanka, would put on a tape of Steven Levine's meditation instructions and leave. There I sat, my right foot on top of my left calf, my back more or less straight, trying to follow the simple instructions. Each week, about halfway into the forty-five minute tape, my knees started to burn. From there on, I stopped hearing the instructions, and I suffered. I hated the pain and just wanted it to stop. I couldn't focus on my breath and I couldn't focus on my pain. I just wanted to move, but I was determined to be a "good meditator" and remain still. I was sure that if I could just get my knees to stop hurting, my meditation would be great.

The weeks went by, and I continued practicing—and suffering. In November I signed up for a five-day retreat with the same monk. I was certain that five days of sitting cross-legged would stretch out whatever needed stretching, and I'd have no more pain. I was destined to be disappointed.

On the retreat I tried piling zafu upon zafu until I was sitting like a prince above the rest of the group. But the pain, and my struggle continued.

Through this all I heard the teaching on working with pain, to focus on the sensations, but I couldn't bring myself to really look. I was too scared.

The next retreat I took, on President's Day weekend, I persisted. By Sunday night, while the rest of the group was wrapped in blankets and shawls, I wore a t-shirt and sweated. I was determined to work through the fire in my knees.

It wasn't until my third retreat that something changed. There, in the High Desert of Southern California, I finally was able to relax and just feel the sensations without flinching—at least for a few seconds. And it was in this process that something remarkable happened: my mind went quiet. Holding my attention on the sensations without trying to push them away had refined my concentration to the point that my first experience of meditative stillness came over me. How ironic, it seemed, that the way into the most pleasant of meditative experiences for me had been the most unpleasant.

Does this mean you have to be a masochist to be a Buddhist? Is this some kind of sick joke or some crazy cult? I come to meditation for some psycho-spiritual healing, and wind up meditating on pain?

Of course Buddhism isn't about hurting ourselves. The Buddha said he taught "suffering and the end of suffering," so obviously these teachings are meant to bring us to a place of some relief, not leave us immersed in pain. But pain is part of the process for many people. At the end of one long retreat I was complaining about the difficulty of sitting still with the sensations in my knees, and a friend said, "I wish I had had pain. I kept falling asleep, and a little pain might have helped me wake up." As one teacher says, "It's always something." For some people it's physical pain, for others it's sleepiness; for some it's childhood trauma or depression, for others it's anxiety or stress. And for some it's addiction.

The point is that meditation—and life—involves difficulties. Learning to hold those difficulties with awareness, compassion, and balance is a vital process of the path. Pushing away these experiences is what addicts do. And, in fact, many other people live the same way. Even as we say, on the one hand, that life is the most precious thing, we are trying to avoid certain aspects of it. To be fully alive means to hold the difficulties, to be fully with them, as well as the pleasures. Otherwise we are only living part of life.

Why Work with Pain?

While pain is an inevitable part of life, sitting with it, with no distractions can make it seem worse. Somehow, in those circumstances, sensations that ordinarily would be below the radar are thrown into relief and can seem intolerable—the subtle itch, the minor throb, the trivial twinge. Even if we aren't experiencing actual pain, these non-threatening occurrences can make it tough to sit still, much less focus the mind. So even if we don't have a lot of pain in practice or don't see a particular need to address it, working with sensations in a skillful way is often a gateway into deepening our practice, through focusing our concentration, revealing hidden physical and emotional patterns, strengthening our ability to be present with difficult emotions, keeping us awake and alert, and strengthening compassion and the ability to be present for the pain of others. I want to talk about how working with sensations accomplishes all these things.

Concentration - One of the most common complaints from meditators is the difficulty in developing concentration. At the beginning and intermediate stages of practice meditators often express frustration about their inability to hold their minds still. And one of the main things that helps concentration is keeping the body still. One formula for this says, "stillness of the body supports stillness of the mind." And it's difficult to keep the body still.

Stillness is not a natural action (or maybe I should say, *inaction*). Even when we are asleep we move. If you pay attention to your body through the day, you will see that just about every physical movement is a response to some kind of discomfort or craving, physical or mental. (As I write this, I ask myself if my typing is included in this claim. In some sense, yes, because I am writing this with the inner struggle of trying to communicate something.) Even as we come to the end of an exhalation, there is the slight craving to be filled with air again. This, in the most basic sense, is what the Buddha meant when he talked about *dukkha,* the pervasive unsatisfactoriness or suffering of life that the First Noble Truth describes. Keeping the body still evokes *dukkha*. This sets up the conflict between our desire for comfort and our desire to deepen our mental stillness. And here we have reached the essential challenge of the spiritual path: to place our search for truth before our search for pleasure. When faced with the task of sitting still in meditation this challenge is set up in the starkest of terms: putting our determination to develop concentration before our moment-to-moment physical comfort.

As we begin to settle into this work, letting the sensations come and go without reacting to them, we counter our innate restlessness. In my experience, at first the restlessness is dominant, sending the mind, and my focus, round and round, never being able to stop and just be with any one moment's experience clearly; but, sooner or later, when I don't react to the discomfort and the restlessness, something happens. My attention draws in closer to whatever is happening, and calm and concentration start to push back and dominate the restlessness. This describes the most basic way in which stillness helps us deepen our practice. When sensations get stronger, the challenge gets greater, but the rewards also grow.

With intense sensations, we're called on to make an even deeper commitment to practice. Now the pain is undeniable. It's not just a matter of subtle sensations being amplified by stillness, but much more intense burning or tightness or heaviness, often triggered by longer periods of meditation. Trying to ignore these sensations is impractical. We need a strategy for opening to them, and, naturally enough, that strategy means deepening our mindfulness. When we can surrender to this process, we discover the hidden jewel of strong sensations, their ability to focus the mind in the most powerful way. While the sensations of breath (a typical meditation object) are subtle and can be difficult to feel, a strong sensation in the back or knee, or anywhere else, is easy to feel and can hold the attention very strongly. Initially, as was true for me, moving our attention deeply into strong sensations can be quite difficult, but the rewards are great. (I'll talk more about how to work with this process later.)

Equanimity - As we begin to work with pain in our practice, some of our underlying tendencies may be revealed. The addictive habits of avoidance, fear, resentment, craving, and clinging are thrown into relief.

In my late teens and early twenties I was something of a pill freak. For a time I carried a little gym bag stuffed with rattling vials. I enjoyed the mania of amphetamines, staying up all night talking, talking, talking, or playing my guitar for hours and hours. I'd found that barbituates and sedatives like Quaalude mimicked, or even enhanced an alcohol high. I had a stash of tranquilizers and anti-depressants stolen from my mother's medicine cabinet just for mixing and matching. I also carried any pain relievers I could get a hold of, like Darvon or codeine. I used these, along with pot, alcohol, and various psychedelics to try to maintain a constant, perfect high. Feeling a little sleepy? Pop a dexadrine. Too hyper? Drop some seconal. Bored or dull mood? Mix a few things together and see what you got. This behavior was an exaggerated form of the natural tendency to avoid pain and seek pleasure.

When I started to meditate it was as though I were being introduced to myself for the first time. "So this is what it feels like to be me?" I'd devoted so much time and energy to trying to fix my reality, to adjust my feelings, to control my mind/body state, that I'd never really seen my experience directly or clearly.

As I started to look closely at the experience of pain, I began to wonder what it was all about. Certainly it was unpleasant, but why was there such a primal response to it? In group interviews with meditation teachers, I saw that the first thing that always seemed to come up was questions about pain. "How do I make it go away?" "Why does my body hurt?" "Is there something wrong with me?" "Isn't there an easier way to practice?"

I could see that there was some fundamental resistance to actually feeling pain. As I began to let go of that resistance, its source became clearer. In my next retreat, my first teacher interview was with a group of fellow meditators and the same questions as always came up. The teacher, whom I had never met before, took a different tack from the usual one of suggesting people just be present with their pain or relax around it. Instead she asked, "What is the *process* of pain?" This seemed to stump the group, but it was a question whose answer I thought I knew.

"Fear of death," I said.

The teacher nodded, but the rest of the students balked. She explained, as I had come to see, that pain is a protective response for the body which is meant to keep us safe, to protect us from danger. It is a survival tool, one that is trying to keep us alive. Pain is a signal to the mind that death may be near, and, since the main instinct of the mind is survival, this threat triggers fear. If we learn to catch the fear and see it clearly, then there is only sensation, and sensation is manageable. What sends us into a spin of restlessness and aversion, is the fear that our lives are threatened. In meditation we have to train ourselves not to be fearful, or perhaps more accurately, not to be reactive to fear. This is why the spiritual path is sometimes called the path of a warrior. The courage involved in facing the physical and mental demons is like that required by the warrior facing death on the battlefield.

As we learn to hold strong sensations in this new way, other qualities develop as well. The non-reactivity needed to simply be present with the sensations brings equanimity to the mind. This quality of balance is treasured in the Buddhist tradition as the essence of the Middle Way, neither moving towards or away from any experience, neither grasping nor rejecting. Far from being a neutral state, equanimity is exalted. Where there is no fear, there is serenity and faith; where there is no grasping, there is contentment.

When working with pain, we might ask which came first, the equanimity or the letting go of fear and resistance. As I sit with pain—and it's never easy—I watch this process. Before the concentration and equanimity come, there's a restlessness and frustration. I don't want to go through this, I don't want to feel it. I know there is another side I can get to, but I want to be there *now*. I try to let go of resistance, I try to breathe into the pain, I try to develop my equanimity, to find my center. And when this transition happens, it all seems to happen at once. It seems that the letting go and the developing happen together. Perhaps they are the same thing, or else they depend on each other. I don't know. This is one of the mysteries of practice for me.

With equanimity, it becomes possible to be more present with all kinds of difficult experiences. When I started to conquer my fear of physical pain in meditation, I thought I was making a lot of progress—and I was—but that success was relatively trivial compared to the next challenge I faced: overcoming my fear of emotional pain. I thought that my practice was deepening, but couldn't understand why there was a certain dullness to it. My teachers quickly recognized that I was holding back from letting emotional pain into my awareness and began to prod me to open to this as well.

I struggled trying to locate these subtle feelings, and as I did I once again felt that I was meeting a part of myself that had been hidden from me for my whole life. Just as with physical pain, I had always pushed away emotional pain. Clearly my drug and alcohol addictions were manifestations of this. That resistance manifested in many other ways as well, such as running from relationships that started to become the least difficult; avoiding professional challenges that might threaten my self-esteem; and viewing depression as tragic and romantic rather than seeing it clearly as a pathology needing treatment.

Introducing myself to my emotions was part of the long, slow process that in the Twelve Step world we call "recovery," and in Buddhism, "waking up." As usual, my expectation was of some quick fix, as though just by feeling my emotions I'd be "cured" of any dysfunction. Instead I simply gained access to the lifelong process of being present with what is, with what I am feeling. Being present is not a "cure" for life, or *dukkha*, but it is the beginning of finding wholeness.

Understanding Pain

The first time I experienced pain with clarity on a retreat, when the thoughts and resistance dropped away and I just relaxed into the sensations, I realized that pain wasn't what I thought it was. If these sensations that I'd always thought were bad and unacceptable could actually help me concentrate, and, indeed, could be experienced as something altogether different, then I would have to re-think my understanding of what pain was. And over time, as I explored this question, certain deeper truths came to light, truths that were beyond my personal experience and pointed to some of the universal truths taught by the Buddha, what we can call the dharma of pain.

It's All Relative - The first truth that became evident was that pain is relative. The same sensation can be experienced as an unacceptably unpleasant feeling or as just a conglomeration of tingling qualities. The difference is dependent not on the sensation itself, but on my mind state when experiencing the sensation. If pain in my knee could lead to a calm, peaceful mind state and (eventually) dissolve completely into rapture, then how could I even define it as unpleasant, much less painful?

Before I go any further with this idea, I want to make clear some important distinctions. One way to view sensations is to see them existing on a continuum. The continuum moves from extreme pleasure to extreme pain. At the extremes most of us will not be able to maintain any balance or see the relative nature of the sensations. But as we move toward the middle of the continuum, things become much more difficult to classify. So, I don't mean to imply that absolutely any sensation should be held with such equanimity. But, I will suggest that many more sensations are ambiguous in nature and potentially less of a problem than we normally think. (Strictly speaking, the early Buddhist texts say that an enlightened one can maintain equanimity even as his/her limbs are cut off, but, even if the Buddha meant this literally, it's a level of mental/spiritual development that is so far out of reach for most of us as to be irrelevant to this discussion.)

To make the relativity of pain more evident, think about the sensations you feel when you eat spicy food. Many people consider this experience to be pleasant, and will go out of their way to get the hottest seasoning available. Now, consider if you had the same sensation in your knee. You'd be complaining about how much it hurt. Sensation in your mouth? Yum. In your knee? Ouch. This is an obvious example of the relativity of pain.

Another great example is the sensations that appear in a rigorous workout. If you were sitting still and your lungs started to burn and your legs started to feel heavy and tired, you would be alarmed. If you were near the end of a five mile run, you would know this was normal, and might even enjoy the sense of stretching your limits.

A final, perhaps strange example is orgasms. The sensations associated with sexual release are considered some of the most pleasurable we can have. But if you felt those sensations in your ear or your toe, you'd call a doctor—maybe even go to the emergency room. If we focus purely on the physical sensations of orgasm there is often, I think, some pain in there.

It's this relativity that leads meditation teachers to refer to "sensations" rather than pain. It makes sense to use a more neutral word—a sensation is always a sensation, but whether it's pain or not can vary.

What does it mean that pain is relative? It means that when there's a sensation in the body, even an apparently unpleasant one, we don't have to react negatively towards it. We understand that our perception of that sensation is conditioned by many factors, and that it might be possible to change that conditioning. In my early days of practice when knee pain would start to appear, my breath would get tight, my body tense and I'd have a sense of dread, even despair as I would pull away from the sensations. Nowadays I often (though not always) find myself drawn right into the sensations. My breath deepens, taking in the sensations themselves, my body relaxes more, rather than getting tense, and my attention deepens into the experience. I'm able to react in this way because fundamentally I understand that sensations are largely what I make of them. They are a problem if I make them a problem. Again, though, I want to emphasize that this kind of equanimity is only possible for me in the milder cases of sensation, and in non-chronic pain. (I'll talk about chronic pain later.)

The Dharmas of Pain - Besides the truth of the relativity of pain, there are three other dharmas of pain relevant to the Buddhist teachings: *dukkha*, *anicca*, and *anatta*, or suffering, impermanence, and no-self. These three are called the "Three Characteristics (or Marks) of Existence." They are also seen as the gateways to insight, the truths that when explored and understood on the deepest level usher in awakening.

I've already talked a lot about suffering, but there are a couple other things worth saying. On the most fundamental level, insight into suffering around pain is the realization that it is normal, that it is a natural part of life, not an aberration. Often when we feel pain there's the thought, "why is this happening to me?" Of course, pain is often a sign of a physical problem, and that is the obvious answer to the question. But the more accurate answer, as I told someone recently who asked if I knew what had caused some back problems I was having, is "I have a body." If I have a body, I will have pain, that's just the way it is. Seeing that, accepting that, is a huge part of developing the equanimity to be with sensations without making them a problem. Understanding *dukkha* as a natural part of life allows us to see the world and its sorrows and pains in a different light. This insight actually helps foster the "coolness" that is nirvana. The Buddha goes further than just saying I suffer because I have a body; he says that I suffer because I was born. This might seem obvious to the point of absurdity, but it actually opened him to his ultimate goal, not to be reborn. In the traditional teachings the Buddha says that one who is fully enlightened ceases to be reincarnated, and thus gets off the wheel of suffering. Ultimately, this is the only way to end all suffering. Many contemporary commentators take this teaching more metaphorically, saying that if our ego isn't reborn moment to moment, then we won't suffer. This is a lot more palatable a teaching to many skeptical contemporary Westerners. And maybe that's what he meant. And, indeed, if my level of awakening allows me to have my limbs cut off without suffering, then I may transcend suffering in this lifetime. Otherwise, the Buddha's teaching that the only way to eliminate all suffering is to stop coming back in a body makes a lot of sense.

The second characteristic of existence, impermanence, is the one I apply most in the moment of experiencing strong sensations. One of the first things I learned when I began to explore pain was that it wasn't the solid mass I'd always thought it was. When the attention becomes refined and we are able to relax and just feel what's going on, pain is in constant movement, constant change. This continual flux is true of all physical sensations. This seemingly solid thing we call our body is really not solid at all, it really has no permanence. When we close our eyes and begin to move the attention through the body what we find is these widely varying sensations. The hands feel one way, the back another, and the face something else entirely. And it's all a roiling mass of effervescent sensation—what we call "life."

On the most obvious level, this insight can help us to hang in when there is pain: "It will pass. I can get through this." This is not an insignificant fact. There is such a tendency of the mind to think that what is happening now will always be happening, that it takes some fairly transforming experiences to break that habit of thought. When we bring the attention over and over and deeper and deeper into awareness of this continual experience of changing sensations in the body, we are chipping away at this illusion of impermanence. The heart and mind are gradually trained to respond to life in a new way, in a way that understands that "this too shall pass."

As concentration deepens in our exploration of sensations, the experience of impermanence opens us to the deeper truth of the insubstantiality of the body--*anatta*. The body is not anybody. Huh? What I mean is that, if something is in a constant state of flux, ungraspable, not solid, then what is its identity? Identity relies on something solid, something stable that can be identified, but the body is neither solid nor stable. This truth of insubstantiality, of corelessness, is the heart of Buddhist insight. If there is no solid body, no solid self, then there is no one to cling, and since clinging is the cause of suffering, this realization, when it occurs on the deepest level, can end suffering. This is what the Buddha said. When spoken, or written, this idea might seem frightening or bizarre, or just plain ridiculous. The Buddha didn't expect us to accept this idea because he said it was so. He suggested that we explore our experience for ourselves and see if it aligned with what he was saying. It really does us no good to intellectually accept or reject the teaching of no-self.

Meditation: Working with Pain

I've already described, at least in passing, much of the approach to working with pain, but I want to take you through, as best I can, the specifics in an orderly way. As with all meditation instruction, however, you will have to work with these suggestions yourself to find your own way of dealing with sensations.

In the vipassana practice, one of the most useful techniques is the noting practice I've described in which you make soft mental notes of each experience as it arises, starting with "In, out" or "rising, falling" to note the breath, then noting "thinking, thinking," "hearing, hearing," and with sensations "sensation, sensation." (I'm not sure why it's suggested that we repeat the word, but it does have the effect of both confirming what's happening and making it impersonal.) It's suggested that we *don't* make the note "pain, pain," because that can create more resistance and discomfort, and besides, as we've already seen, the same sensation might be called pain or pleasure depending on our mind state and the cause of the sensation. So, one of the first things we can do when a strong sensation arises is to note it. This doesn't mean we just glance at it or try to dismiss it with the note, but rather that we are facing the sensation squarely.

As we do this, it's important to soften, to relax the body in the area of the sensation. Use the breath, especially the out-breath, to relax. Much of the difficulty with strong sensations comes from the tightening and tension that occurs in reaction to the sensation. If we can soften, we won't amplify the sensation. The tightening is both a protective mechanism of the body and an expression of the fear that arises with strong sensations. Breathe into the sensations. As we counteract this resistance, we are brought into the direct presence of the sensation—we're noting it, not resisting it, just allowing it to be.

It is at this point that we begin to apply the central tool of vipassana meditation: mindfulness. We take the attention into the sensation, exploring it with a scientific curiosity. What is this? What does this feel like? Where in the body is the sensation most intense? Where is its center? Its outer boundary? What qualities does it contain? In the traditional teachings, we use the four elements, earth, air, water, and fire, as frames of reference for sensations. Heaviness or denseness is an expression of the earth element; pulsing, tingling, flowing, or any movement is the air element; heat or coolness is the fire element; and fluidity and cohesiveness are the water element. Using the elements helps us to categorize the sensations and to see them as impersonal manifestations of the material world—all physical objects are said to be made up of varying amounts of the elements. We can use these descriptions or whatever works for us. We can make mental notes of the qualities of the sensations or we can just be aware of the changing qualities. The point is to take an objective, non-reactive approach to experiencing the sensations.

As we keep paying attention to the sensations we need to be kind to ourselves. Be careful that you aren't creating a hardcore relationship to the sensations. Keep coming back to the relaxation part. And keep breathing. The breath is an important tool here. If aversion starts to slip in--tension, resistance, frustration, sadness, self-pity--come back to the breath. Maybe take a deep breath and release—softening again around the strong sensations.

As the meditation period goes on a variety of things may happen. At a certain point, the aversion may overwhelm your mindfulness so that you are just caught in suffering with no space or equanimity around the experience. If you find that you truly can't get centered again, that you don't have the power of mind right then to apply mindfulness and calm, it might be time to move the body. When we move in meditation, what's important is to do so slowly and mindfully. There's no reason that the shift in posture can't be incorporated as a part of the meditation. One way to emphasize this is to put the hands into prayer position for a moment before moving, a sort of bow and acknowledgement that you are about to move. Then, slowly and with great attention on the sensations in the body, change posture. There are some postures that are almost as solid as the cross-legged posture that can be used as your secondary posture. Explore for yourself (beforehand) a good secondary posture that you can move into when necessary. If you just break posture without a stable secondary posture to go to, you are likely to lose the thrust of your meditation.

After you move, check through the body again and see how the sensations have changed. Look at the mind and emotions to see how they have changed as well. Then try to settle back into the body, relaxing, and beginning again to follow the breath. You are starting your sitting again now. You likely will have lost a degree of concentration, so you need to pay attention to any restlessness or disturbance and try to bring calm back. You might also take a moment to enjoy the end of the painful sensations.

Dangers of Working with Pain

Because there's such a strong tendency to want to move away from pain, to escape it or ignore it or relieve it, I think it's important in meditation to take a different approach, the approach I've been describing. However, pain *is* an expression of some kind of problem in the body, and as such we need to be very careful in working with it. There are a few things I would suggest that you keep in mind as you work with pain.

First, as I mentioned before, people who are very determined in their meditation practice can start to take on a hardcore approach, pushing themselves harder and harder. While this kind of intensity certainly has its value, it can get us into trouble around pain. Physically it can cause us to overburden the body, straining muscles, tendons, and ligaments to the point of injury. Although this is extremely rare, it has happened. If the pain doesn't dissipate during the sitting, and/or if it remains afterward, you may be overdoing it. Ask yourself, and ask your teacher or trusted friend, if you seem to be over-striving in your practice. Try backing off in your effort.

Although it's rare, it is possible to override the body's natural warning systems with mindfulness. One friend who was suffering from a rare blood disease had developed his mindfulness of sensations so deeply that he was able to function in a very weakened physical state. When he finally decided to seek medical help and *rode his bicycle* to the emergency room the doctors told him that, based on his blood count, he should have been flat on his back. They were amazed that he could walk, much less ride a bike. While this story certainly shows the power of the practice—the power of mind over body—it also is a cautionary tale about not listening to what the body actually needs. It's important to use common sense in practice and not become so singlemindedly devoted to a very narrow kind of mindfulness that we lose the big picture of what is really happening.

Mentally, this kind of effort can create more blockage. The striving itself, the competitive attitude, is counter to the meditative attitude of just watching. The Third Zen Patriarch says, "When you try to stop activity to achieve passivity your very effort fills you with activity." So, striving in meditation is a contradiction in terms—and in means. Instead of deepening our practice we can create agitation. Instead of accepting what arises in each moment, we try to control our experience, chasing after some ideal meditative state. Right Effort is not striving and it is not giving up. It is a balance that Suzuki Roshi calls "the secret of practice." And this is a secret that we have to discover for ourselves. It's not a secret that someone is keeping from us, but rather something within us that can only be found through trial and error, through striving too hard, and not making enough effort, swinging back and forth until we find the "Middle Way." And, in truth, even this place of balance will keep changing for us, moment to moment, so that the effort we make needs to constantly be monitored and adjusted to fit the energetic conditions of each moment.

Finally, if we become too focused on painful sensations in practice it can become overwhelming, undermining our confidence in our selves, in our ability to practice, and in the practice itself, making us question the value of a practice that seems to be all about pain. We can lose the joyful part of practice. If this happens, we can develop an aversion to the practice itself and pull away. If these kinds of experiences start to happen, it's important to dial-down our effort and our focus on pain. Find a more comfortable posture; sit in a chair or even lie down; do shorter periods of meditation. Don't let your practice become one continuous grind of fighting with the body. This will only alienate you and weaken your practice.

Living with Chronic Pain

I've been talking about a particular kind of pain, especially the kind that comes from sitting still with our legs crossed or sitting in a chair for long periods of time. This kind of pain is not indicative of any structural problem in the body or of a disease or illness. By and large, this kind of pain dissipates as soon as we stop meditating and move the body. I think that what I've said about working with this kind of pain is accurate, and I hope, helpful. However, it's vital that we distinguish this kind of pain from the pain that indicates real problems in the body, and especially that we understand that chronic pain is very different from "meditation pain."

I would define chronic pain as difficult sensations that appear daily for a period of at least several weeks. A surprisingly high number of people experience this kind of pain, and very often for much longer than a few weeks. Anything can trigger such pain, over-exercise (many athletes have chronic pain), a car or other kind of accident, a chronic illness like cancer, MS, or Chronic Fatigue, or just plain aging (probably the most common cause). When it comes to this kind of pain, we should be cautious about suggesting simple answers like, "just be aware of the sensations" as we might with meditation pain. When pain is persistent it has a debilitating emotional effect.

One of the first differences between the two types of pain is that with chronic pain, it *is* indicative of an actual physiological problem. This has broad implications. First of all, it means that the fear that arises with the pain has more of a basis. It's not just instinctive; it is rational. We have to think about solutions. And we have to be very careful. Especially for addicts and alcoholics, this takes us into dangerous territory.

One friend who had been sober for many years began to have severe nerve pain. Nothing he tried helped. As he became more and more discouraged he slipped into despair and eventually started drinking again. No longer able to work, battling with his wife, his life fell apart. Fortunately he was able to find his way back to a Twelve Step program and overcome the pain problem. Many others are not so lucky.

Sometimes we get into trouble by accident. An older woman friend told me she became addicted to Vicodin when dealing with some pain. "I didn't know it was addictive," she said. I recently had my own bouts with chronic pain and used Vicodin for the first time in my life. I immediately saw the seduction. As a recovering addict, a drug like that just made me feel "normal," relaxed and in a good mood. Although it didn't take the pain away completely, it did dull it. The temptation to keep taking it was there—I was in pain on a daily basis, so it seemed justifiable. But I could see that what really attracted me wasn't the pain relief but the pleasant high. I decided that only when the pain got very severe would I take it, which meant that I used it just a few times over the course of a couple months of pain.

One of the difficulties with chronic pain is that everyone you meet will give you advice. I became so barraged with options for treatment that I became confused and frustrated: chiropractor, acupuncture, physiatrist, osteopath, physical therapy, herbs, drugs, injections, operations. It seemed that every practitioner had a different way of viewing my problem and a different solution. I realized that, ultimately, I was on my own. It came back to trusting myself. What made sense to me? What seemed to be working? I needed to be patient and let a treatment work, but I didn't want to stick with something out of habit or fear or hope. The pain would seem to be getting better, then there'd be a setback. One treatment would seem to help, but I'd find it only took me so far. The fear that I'd never get free of this pain started to grip me. With all of this, I needed mindfulness. I needed to be mindful of the pain, mindful of my reaction to the pain, mindful of my biases for treatment, my resistance to advice, my illusions about magical recovery. All of it.

Then I talked to a friend who had been struggling with her own chronic illness who said sometimes mindfulness itself didn't seem that helpful, that she needed to take her attention *away* from the pain in order to live with it.

When I talked to one of my teachers, he said that I should open to the fear that the pain would never go away. Just allow that thought in—don't push it away. That suggestion had no appeal to me, although I understood the reasoning. The aversion, the resistance to the pain is just adding a layer of difficulty. Allowing for the possibility that the pain won't go away lets me stop running and just be in the situation as it is.

What's clear about chronic pain is that there's no quick fix and that I'm going to have to bring all my resources, inner and outer, to bear in dealing with it. As I age, my body becomes less and less reliable. Learning to live with this, with the inevitability of sickness, old age, and death is one of the central tasks of the Buddhist practitioner. Not to be overcome with despair and not to live in denial—this is the challenge. Everyday I seek that balance of mind that allows me to be present with ease and awareness. Some days I find it, and some days I don't.

There is more, much more, to be learned from pain. It isn't my goal to explain everything there is to know (even if I knew everything there is to know). I only want to inspire you to engage with sensations—with pain—in a new way. Your wisdom will grow through experience, not through reading or thinking about it. Take the tools of practice and apply them with faith, with courage, and with careful attention. What you discover will transform you.

Step Eight

"Made a list of all persons we had harmed, and became willing to make amends to them all."

What's This Step About?

Steps Eight and Nine are the amends Steps, where we actually try to make restitution for the harm we did as addicts. Where the previous Steps were primarily involved with looking inward, now the focus goes out, to our relationships. If we've been fully practicing the previous Steps, we've already started to change the way we relate with people, becoming more honest, caring, and selfless. Now, though, we are faced with the specifics of how we harmed others and what we can do about it.

In *One Breath at a Time*, my first book, I talked about my first experience of practicing Forgiveness and Lovingkindness meditation. What struck me in that experience was how the people I felt the most love for were the same ones I hurt the most—and who hurt me. I suppose that intimacy and the vulnerability that comes with it makes hurting each other easy. For those who are insecure, being close can feel dangerous at times; we easily feel threatened and defensive, striking out at those who are close to us. Many addicts struggle with intimate relationships, even as we feel a desperate need for love.

And so, Step Eight begins this key element of recovery. For us to fulfill the promise of Buddhism and the Steps to find freedom, we must take on this final stage of recovery, healing our past relationships as best we can, and changing the way we approach our new ones. Without these changes, it will be very difficult to maintain our recovery, and our lives will certainly never achieve their potential for happiness.

While no element of the Eightfold Path explicitly correlates to this Step, certainly Right Speech and Right Action, which are all about the way we live and interact in the world, would suggest the wisdom of making amends. And, of course, the Buddhist practices of lovingkindness and forgiveness do tie directly to these Steps.

Stay in the Moment

It's difficult to start making the Step Eight list without looking forward to Step Nine: "How am I ever going to face him?" you might think. "What can I do to make up for that?" or "How am I going to afford to pay her back?" The answer to all these questions and any worries about Step Nine are, "Wait." Step Eight is a separate process from Step Nine, that's why it has its own number. Step Eight is making a list and becoming willing. That's all. Don't make it more than that, or you will miss the real value of the Step. Like many other Steps, Step Eight has a hidden value that is only revealed if you follow the instructions and stay in the moment. Pretend you don't know what the next Step is, and see how that affects the way you do this Step. You may be surprised by the results.

But. . .

When we start to make our list, we'll almost surely have the thought at some point, "But they hurt me, too," or perhaps, "But they hurt me worse," or "But they started it." All of these things may be true, and none of them have anything to do with Step Eight. It can be hard for us to accept, but whether others harmed us or not, we are still responsible for the ways we harmed them. Striking back from a real or perceived injury is still striking back.

The Buddha says that for his true followers, even if their limbs are being sawed off one by one, a thought of hatred will not arise in the mind. Of course, to me this sounds crazy, and I don't know if he meant it literally, but obviously he has strong ideas about how perfectly loving we need to be in order to fulfill his teachings. Perhaps the wisdom in this guidance is the understanding that someone who would saw off your limbs must be so filled with hatred that they are suffering deeply and are deserving of our compassion.

Exercise: The List

The Eighth Step list is usually drawn from our Fourth Step inventory. If the inventory was thorough, we should have plenty of names of people we harmed in our addiction. Of course, we might think of other people we harmed after we complete the inventory, and we shouldn't hesitate to add them to the list.

For this exercise, once you've written the list, reflect on each name and how you harmed them. Look at the roots of your behavior. Did it come out of fear, confusion, self-centeredness, anger, or some other emotion?

Look too at the list in general terms. Who are these people? Do they include family, lovers, and friends? Are they really enemies? Business associates, creative partners, or associates? What do you learn by seeing these patterns? What types of relationships seem to be the most troubling or difficult for you? Seeing these patterns will help you lay a new foundation moving forward in recovery.

Exercise: More Willingness

Once again, Step Eight demands willingness, or "Right Intention." By separating the intention from the action, the Steps make the same distinction as Buddhism, that our motivation needs to be clear and skillful in order for our actions to be successful.

Facing those we harmed is frightening. Admitting a mistake is difficult for anyone, but when the mistakes were as broad-ranging and hurtful as those of an addict, it can be downright overwhelming. So, we take it slowly, writing the list, looking at it, contemplating it, and imagining the process.

Once we've begun the inventory, we have set ourselves on a course that must be completed. Otherwise we will live with unresolved guilt and shame. If we have truly embraced the Step process up to now, we will see that we must throw ourselves into this Step, and it's probably best not to wait. In fact, for many people, Step Five was quickly followed by Six through Nine. You don't want to sit around thinking about it too much. Just do it.

Remember, willingness to make amends doesn't actually mean you are going to make amends to every person on your list. Not that this gives you an out, but the truth is, for a variety of reasons, you probably will not make direct amends to all of them.

Once you've made your list, take some time to visualize and remember each of the people. Remember how you hurt them; feel what it feels like to remember that, to face the guilt and shame of your past. Breathe and accept yourself, knowing that the past is gone, and that the "new you" deeply regrets your behavior. This is the beginning of forgiveness.

Becoming a Person Who. . .

Recently I heard someone in a meeting describe how she thought the Steps work. She said that the Steps helped her to "become a person who . . ." and then she described various changes, like Step Three helped her become a person who accepts things and turns them over.

I found this an important way to view the Steps because oftentimes the Steps seem to be viewed as a mechanical process whereby we perform a single action, and then we're done with the Step. And, while it's true that there are some useful functions of simply going through the Steps, what this woman was pointing to was the importance of *living* the Steps, of, essentially, becoming a different person—or at least a different *version* of the person you were.

For me, the middle Steps, 4-9, are about becoming a person who takes responsibility for one's actions. Addicts want to blame the world, their parents, their lovers, their kids, their bosses, politicians, the economy, the weather—you name it. Anything but themselves. It seems to be the most difficult thing for addicts to simply admit they are wrong or that they are sorry or should have behaved differently. This isn't the same as the constant apologizing that some addicts fall into, "I'm sorry," following every misstep, followed by the next misstep. That isn't taking responsibility, but simply feeling guilty and wanting to be exonerated without actually changing.

Taking responsibility is about seeing clearly our own failings and sincerely trying to change.

Step Nine

"Made direct amends to such people wherever possible, except when to do so would injure them or others."

What's This Step About?

We've arrived at a Step that many of us looked to with great trepidation, but if we've done the work of the previous Steps thoroughly, perhaps we'll be able to face this Step with at least a little less anxiety. Clearly, Step Nine is about trying to somehow make up for the harm we've done in our lives. It must be a rare addict who arrives at this Step with no work to do. Certainly most, if not all, of us have harmed many people in our lives. But one thing needs to be clear: we can't go back and fix all the harm we've done. And we can't make amends to everyone we've hurt. For one thing some of the people might be dead or long gone from our lives, and for another, as the Step suggests, for some people, just bringing up the past or confessing our mistakes will create more harm than it will heal.

This truth then, the limits of our amends, points to another fundamental fact about this Step: it's not about actually making amends to everyone. Yes, there will be some amends that we really need to make and that may even heal longstanding wounds and alienation. But more than that, amends is the final stage of honestly confronting and admitting our failures that actually starts in Step One. This is clearly one of the central themes and purposes of the Steps, "rigorous honesty." Admitting we have a problem is a huge first step; admitting the "exact nature of our wrongs," takes us even deeper; and finally, dealing directly with those we harmed forces us to face our failings in a way that probably few people ever do. And the results, as many of us know, are incredibly freeing. Perhaps that's why, in the AA Big Book, the so-called "Promises" appear in Step Nine.

From a Buddhist perspective, I think what's happening here is a tearing down of ego and ego-attachment. If you take all of this personally, the addiction and all the behaviors that came with it, you'll probably never even get through the Steps—in fact, that's one reason many people can't even do Step One. But through the process, especially when paired with attending meetings where we hear others share about all their own misbehaviors, a shift can take place. Instead of seeing our addiction as personal, it starts to seem more generic. Our personal story loses some of its uniqueness as we hear so many others; a skillful sponsor's reaction to our inventory shows us that we didn't do anything that millions of other addicts hadn't done; and by the time we start to make amends, we might not even feel like the same person who did these terrible things. Certainly we should be living our life by completely different principles and values, so that, while we feel bad about what we did, we feel that we are on the road of redemption, that we have truly changed and so don't have to carry the past as so much painful, unresolved baggage.

It's with this spirit that we enter into the process of making amends.

Forgiveness and Compassion

We start the amends process with a list. Here we see the names of all those we've harmed, or at least that we can remember harming. Once again we may feel a heavy heart as we realize the harm we've done. For many of us, the Step and recovery process has awakened a caring and compassion we have rarely felt, and where in the past we might have had callous feelings or dismissed other people's suffering, we now can be touched in a deep way. In the Buddhist tradition there are ritual meditative and contemplative ways to approach our regrets through forgiveness and compassion practices.

Meditation: Forgiveness

Forgiveness meditation starts by connecting with the heart:

- Begin by settling in to a comfortable posture where you can stay alert. Consciously relax with some deeper breaths, releasing any tension in the body.
- Feel the breath in the center of the chest, the Heart Center, and have a sense of softening and opening in that place.
- Once you've settled in for perhaps 3-5 minutes, begin to work with the following imagery and phrases. The three aspects of forgiveness, forgiving ourselves, forgiving others, and asking forgiveness, can be done in any order that works for you. I present self-forgiveness first because it's so often the most difficult for people.
- **Forgiving ourselves**: begin by contemplating all the ways that you harmed yourself, internally and externally. This of course includes your addictive behavior, but also ways that you gave up on yourself, whether in school, in a relationship, or in a job. How have you talked to yourself or viewed yourself in negative terms. Self-hatred is a common disease in our culture, especially

among addicts, and the truth is, as human beings, we don't deserve to be hated. Repeat these phrases to yourself: *For all the ways I have harmed myself through thought, word, and deed, I forgive myself. I forgive myself.* We may not feel anything right away, but it's important to stay with this process, and not just in a single sitting, but to keep coming back to this process over time until the tightness in the heart starts to break up and we begin to have a sense of self-forgiveness.

- **Forgiving others**: resentments are sometimes called "the number one killer" for addicts, and certainly, many of us carry longterm anger, blaming, and trauma. Ultimately, this anger harms us as much as it does our enemy. We are the ones who are living with the nagging thoughts and obsessions. To forgive others does not mean we condone their behavior or that we will ever let them hurt us again. It just means that we don't want to carry this baggage with us. Bring to mind the people who have harmed you and the things they've done to you. Breathing into your heart, say to them, *For all the ways you have hurt me through thought, word, or deed, I offer my forgiveness. I forgive you.* Again, we can't expect instant results. But we need to stick with this process. Sometimes there will be a sudden shift or insight, and at others just a gradual melting of the icy heart. Stick with it.

- **Asking Forgiveness**: each of us carries a burden of guilt from our addictive and selfish behaviors. Step Nine is about doing something about those unskillful actions. Forgiveness meditation allows us to do the inner work of accepting forgiveness, whether or not we actually receive it externally. For this part of the exercise, think of the people on your Eighth Step list and the ways you harmed each one. Bring each person to mind and say to yourself, *For all the ways that I hurt you, through thought,* word, or deed, I ask your forgiveness. *Please forgive me.* Again, it can be difficult to accept that we are forgiven, but this is a form of internal amends, admitting responsibility and asking if we can move on.

Work with these three aspects of forgiveness as much and for as long as is necessary. There's no timetable for forgiveness. You may find that you feel that one of the aspects really stands out as needing attention. That's fine. Use the practice in whatever ways feel beneficial to you.

Meditation: Compassion

For compassion practice, we once again focus on the heart. Remember to be creative with this practice. I recommend phrases to use, but you can use anything that works for you.

- Begin by settling into a comfortable posture where you can stay alert. Consciously relax with some deeper breaths, releasing any tension in the body.
- Feel the breath in the center of the chest, the Heart Center, and have a sense of softening and opening in that place.
- Once you've settled in for perhaps 3-5 minutes, begin to work with the following imagery and phrases.
- Bring to mind people you know who are suffering, either physically, emotionally, professionally, or in some other way. As you see them in your mind, say to them, *I care about your pain. May you be free from suffering.* You can use these phrases or make up your own. As you say the phrases, stay in touch with your breath in the heart center. Work with this for several minutes or longer, however long you are able to sustain your sense of connection.
- Now think of yourself and the challenges in your life. Say the phrases to yourself. *I care about my pain. May I be free from suffering.* Stay with your heart, noticing any tendency to dismiss

your own problems or, on the contrary, to indulge in self-pity. Try to stay balanced, caring, but not overwhelmed emotionally.

- Finally, begin to reflect on the suffering of human and other beings throughout the planet. Use phrases like, *I care about the pain of all beings. May all beings be free from suffering.*

- To close, come back to your own heart, body, and breath. Connect with your own feeling of being present. Breathe and have a sense of releasing any burden of suffering you've taken on with this practice.

Wherever Possible

Making amends is perhaps one of the most personal and delicate aspects of the Twelve Steps. Because it's so difficult to be objective about how and to whom to make amends, consulting with a sponsor or spiritual guide before embarking on this process is absolutely vital. So often I have had people ask me if I thought they should make a particular amends, and it would seem obvious to me that they weren't seeing the whole picture.

I want to talk about one particular situation that arises for many of us. When I was 18 months sober and deep into my amends process, I wanted to contact my ex-girlfriend. There had been many ways I'd hurt her, from my anger and violence (to her furniture), to my dishonesty and remoteness. She certainly qualified as someone I had harmed, so she fit the first part of the Step. However, before I could contact her, my sponsor asked me what the likely result of calling her would be. Would it help her? Would it heal her wounds?

This particular relationship had ended with me moving out and she had already made a couple attempts to reconnect. I was clear that I didn't want to be with her anymore, but she hadn't let go.

195

When my sponsor asked me these questions, I realized that contacting her would only arouse hope in her that there was still a chance for us. When I looked at my motives, I could see that they came out of my own guilt and need for absolution. This wasn't the proper intention for making amends. Amends needed to be about the other person, not about me. I had to put this one aside, which was very difficult.

The reverse situation is one that I'm often asked about. Someone says they want to make amends to an ex, but when I inquire, I find out that they are harboring the wish to get back together. This is, of course, completely out of bounds. And yet, if I'm being completely honest, I have to admit that I did this—and it worked out! I had broken up with a girlfriend, and felt that she was to blame for the way our relationship had gone. However, six months later, I had a (painful) realization that the blame largely lay with me, and I badly wanted to get back together. I contacted her to apologize, and by the end of the meeting, I'd asked her out. A year later we were married, and so far, we still are.

I guess the lesson is, "You never know."

Ultimately, one of the most painful parts of the amends process is seeing its limitations. Seeing that we can't make amends to someone we hurt, either because it would hurt them again, because of our own guilt or selfish agenda, or even because they've died, leaves us with a sense of incompletion. Now that we are truly living a different life, we want our past to be cleaned up. And yet, it can't be. And this is the final letting go of this Step. We may start out with trepidation, but by the end, many of us are intrepid in our willingness to do what it takes to complete this process. Once we let go of the fear and embark on this work, we often discover that this deeper letting go is another surprising lesson from the Twelve Steps.

Exercise: Preparing to Make Amends

Before we make amends, we'll want to rehearse a bit. Begin by referring back to the Step Five guidelines for Right Speech: to speak the truth, in a timely manner, and only when useful and kind. This guidance should help us to know when and where to speak and what to say. One of the hard things is to "stay on our side of the street." With many or most amends, the damage went both ways. But we're only responsible for what we did. We need to be very clear that we aren't making amends with the hope of getting an apology back. That's a dangerous attitude. We need to stick to the matter at hand, and remember that we're trying to help the other person. Sometimes, of course, that's going to mean giving them money or at least beginning to pay them back.

Because making amends can be very emotional, it can be helpful to go over in our mind the exact words we plan to say. It's so easy to fall into blaming, excuse making, and all sorts of prevarication, so knowing just what we want to say can help us to stay on message. We also want to choose a time and place that allows for a safe situation. For some amends, it might be better to do them in public, others in private; some should be done face to face, while others are best over the phone or even by letter. All of this should be considered and discussed with a sponsor or spiritual guide. The worst outcome is if an amends goes wrong and creates more damage, and that's always possible when dealing with such delicate relationships and truths.

Exercise: Living Amends

Some amends simply can't be made in a direct way. And some aren't specific to a person. Many of us find that we want to do some form of service as an expression of our humility and regret. This can often take the form of helping an organization or group that is representative of someone or some community we harmed. As we devote our lives to our recovery, we'll probably get lots of opportunities to be of service. The way we live now may be the ultimate form of amends to the world.

Amends to Ourselves

Clearly, making amends to others is a subtle and complex process. We can't always be clear about who we should make amends to. But one person who was there for every mistake, who suffered every time we used, who took the brunt of all our selfish, foolish, and destructive behavior, was us. We are the ultimate owners of our karma, the ones who carry the burden of our past, and as we move forward in our lives and in our recovery, we are the ones we owe the greatest amends to.

Of course, simply getting clean and sober is a huge start in healing our past. But I think that many of us have to learn to be more kind to ourselves. As selfish as we might have been, addicts are also terribly self-destructive and full of self-hatred. While we may have been seeking pleasure in our addictive behavior, we may also have been trying to harm or even kill ourselves. Now we have to learn what might be the hardest lesson: to love ourselves. This is an inside *and* outside job.

Mindfulness teaches us how to see our own thoughts, and this is where our amends begin. We need to listen inside and try to change that voice. We don't have to beat ourselves up or take the negative view on everything. Humility is one thing, but self-abnegation is quite another. The Buddha encouraged us to give love to all beings, *including ourselves.* We are all human and equally valuable. Can we take that in? Can we start to treat ourselves as if we believed that?

Exercise: Amends to Ourselves

Making amends to ourselves starts with getting clean and sober, whatever program or addiction we are working with. True recovery, though, demands that we continue to take care of ourselves through all the challenges and opportunities life presents us.

For this exercise, ask yourself what you are doing for yourself today. More generally, what are you doing for yourself in your life right now. Are you taking care of your body with food, rest, and exercise? Is your work life satisfying? Your family life? Social life? What opportunities do you have for fun and pleasure? Do you have a creative outlet?

Sometimes recovery, or just trying to live a spiritual life can become a kind of grind as we try to live up to some high standards or always do the right thing, be of service, work hard, and be responsible. Sometimes when we get into recovery, a sense of guilt combined with a newfound energy and engagement turns us into workaholics. At one point in early recovery I was working fulltime, leading a band on weekends, and taking classes at night. Then I decided to write a novel. Not surprisingly, soon thereafter my girlfriend broke up with me. She felt abandoned since I didn't have time for her.

It's vital, if we are to sustain our recovery that we be kind to ourselves, that we take time to enjoy ourselves. Just learning how to have fun in recovery is a big challenge for many of us, but an important one to accomplish.

Consider all of this as you move into making amends to yourself.

PART THREE: FULFILLMENT

Steps Ten through Twelve bring us into the realm of living recovery. Now we have embraced the process and want only to continue to grow and fulfill the promises of the path. We are encouraged to look inside with meditation and prayer, and outside, with service and generosity. Here we find the great joy of recovery.

Step Ten

"Continued to take personal inventory and when we were wrong promptly admitted it."

What's This Step About?

Step Ten continues with the theme of self-investigation, honesty, and responsibility. It points to the fact that a one-time inventory isn't enough for our recovery, that we need to live a life of integrity. This, then, begins the theme of the last three Steps, bringing the lessons and practices of the first nine Steps into fruition in our daily lives and making a lifelong commitment to the values of the Steps.

Step Ten can be practiced in many different ways: as a daily ritual review of our behavior; as a quick acknowledgment of a mistake; as a meditative exploration of thought patterns and feelings; or as an ongoing exploration of troubling themes that appear regularly in our lives.

This Step makes even more clear the idea that we are "becoming people who" live the Steps, not just "work" them. Living the Steps means we aren't just following the rules or going through some rote exercises. It means that we've totally bought into the principles of recovery. If the Steps are going to have any real meaning for us, and if we are going to live the life we long for, it's this commitment that's required. Any way that we hold back from embracing this process will undermine our happiness, and ultimately our recovery itself.

Promptly Admitting

The good news about Step Ten is that we don't have to go through the laborious inventory process of Step Four and all the emotions that can come up when confronting our past. Hopefully what we've learned from that process is that we don't want to carry those burdens again, that we don't want to accumulate a long list of mistakes that must be addressed. Instead, as Step Ten tells us, now we can take care of things more or less as they happen.

Hopefully what we've also learned in the Step process is humility. This Step calls on us to draw on humility as a regular part of our makeup. Admitting we are wrong whenever we need to mostly likely means that we will regularly be making amends. We are all imperfect; the Steps remind us of that. This Step requires that we continue to remember and admit that fact.

One of the benefits of such a practice is that it helps us to let go of the attachment to self or ego. If every time we make a mistake we take it personally, we are going to struggle. When we understand that we aren't unique or uniquely flawed but just generic, mistake-ridden humans, there is much less to worry about. This perspective, of course, is what Buddhism encourages.

When we do find ourselves struggling with blows to the ego, that pain itself can act as a wakeup for us, reminding us to be more mindful and to let go of clinging to some image that we think will impress the world. Over time a sense of freedom will come as we become less and less susceptible to the suffering that comes from trying to protect this illusory sense of self. Our interactions, too, will improve as defensiveness fades and honesty and taking responsibility grow.

Exercise: Daily Inventory

Daily inventory is an important ritual for many people in recovery. This is typically done at the end of the day, and can be written or contemplated. We go over the major interactions of the day and ask if we've left any negative residue; we consider our motives for our actions, if they were in harmony with our spiritual values; we look at our inner life, how we treated ourselves through they day.

Having made this kind of review, we consider if there are amends we need to make to anyone. If so, we make a commitment to ourselves to make those amends, including a specific time to do it. If we have some concerns, we resolve to contact our sponsor or other spiritual friend for advice or feedback.

Cognitive Inventory

When I teach meditation I get a lot of questions that relate to dropping or getting rid of thoughts. People want to have a quiet mind during meditation, and find all the thoughts to be troubling. Also, they often judge themselves as bad meditators if they are having a lot of thoughts. However, from the standpoint of spiritual practice, having thoughts during meditation gives an opportunity for growth. As we start to notice our habitual thought patterns, we see how we create our own suffering through regrets, resentments, fears, and judgments. We see how our thoughts trigger stress. We notice our obsessions, where we spend all our mental energy. All of this is vital information that gives us an opportunity to change.

Cognitive therapy, which is especially helpful in treating depression, uses an approach similar to meditative investigation of thoughts. In fact, it's been adapted into a Buddhist-based program called Mindfulness-Based Cognitive Therapy (MBCT) that combines mindfulness meditation with a more focused, clinical treatment. Cognitive therapy is based on the idea that our inaccurate or unrealistic thoughts, called "cognitive distortions," are at the root of depression and anxiety. This therapeutic approach then starts by being aware of these distortions, questioning them, and trying to see things in more realistic terms. You can see how similar this is to basic mindfulness of thoughts meditation.

The insight that triggered the development of MBCT was that, even when people saw their thoughts realistically, if they took them personally, they could continue to judge themselves, if only for having the thoughts in the first place: "I shouldn't have these stupid thoughts," or "What's wrong with me that I keep thinking so negatively?" What MBCT does is take the Buddhist insight into selflessness—the essentially impersonal nature of thoughts, that they aren't me or mine—and add this to the cognitive therapy approach. Now thoughts become simply words and images passing through the mind.

What I appreciate about the MBCT approach, which I've used in my own struggles with depression, is that it puts a special focus on the tools of meditation. Even though for years I practiced mindfulness meditation, when I simply noted thoughts or observed them, I wasn't seeing so clearly the cause and effect relationship between thoughts and moods. I would say that the "goal" of Buddhist meditation isn't so much therapeutic, but more about universal insights leading to a spiritual transformation, while MBCT allows us to focus our practice on something more psychological and emotionally healing. While these two goals can be pursued simultaneously, for me, if I don't take care of myself emotionally, it's very difficult to move into the more spiritual viewpoint because I'm lost in my own stuff.

The cognitive distortions themselves have been categorized in David Burns classic book *Feeling Good*, but for addicts, we can see that they are very familiar forms of extreme thinking: perfectionism, self-judgment and self-hatred, resentment and judgment of others, and seeing everything through a negative lens. We take our feelings to be facts and our thoughts to be truths. If we make a mistake we are failures, and if we have a success, we were just lucky. And finally, it's all about me.

It's this whole thought and emotional structure that has to be torn down for us to experience happiness. That process of deconstruction starts by observing thoughts and feelings and seeing how they form, the whole karmic process. This is what mindfulness of thoughts and feelings reveals, and it's also what the inventory process, both Steps Four and Ten, reveal. Once seen, our whole understanding of what these thoughts and feelings represent needs to be altered. Even if we see their flaws, if we still think they belong to us, then we believe that we are flawed. This puts us in conflict with ourselves, an untenable situation. "I know these thoughts are crazy, but that's who I am." This is why the idea of impersonality is so important. If we watch thoughts and feelings appear and disappear day after day, eventually we may be able to realize that they aren't a true expression of "I." In fact, we'll see that our thoughts and beliefs are so variable and changeable that they couldn't be the expression of a single, solid self because they so often simply disagree with each other. We start to see that they are more like energies that just bubble up out of the mind triggered by conditioning and events, by fatigue or anger, by what others say or what we remember, by work or the news or our last conversation. Sure there are patterns and tendencies that are pretty deeply engrained, but even those don't belong to us. It's like the Zen story of the student coming to the Zen master and saying, "I'm such an angry person. How can I stop being angry?"

The Zen master asks, "Where is your anger now?"

"I'm not angry now," says the student.

Anger comes and goes; it doesn't belong to us. Nothing is permanent, nothing is solid. Right View means keeping this perspective so that we don't get caught up in cognitive distortions or the Wrong View of identity and permanence.

Exercise: Cognitive Inventory

Start looking at your thoughts to detect these types of distorted thinking:

- **All or Nothing**

This is when we see things in extremes, and it's what perfectionism is about. When I was in college, I was maintaining a 4.0 GPA until I encountered a class in statistics. Near the end of the term I was getting a C. I called my sponsor from campus one day in despair and told him I was going to drop the class. He pointed out that I was setting unrealistic expectations of myself—perfection. Besides that, I'd only have to take the class again, throwing away the whole term's work.

I often refer to the book "The Spirituality of Imperfection," because the title itself inspires me. Living with imperfection is what life is about, and certainly what the Buddha talked about. Accepting the Noble Truth of Suffering, just like admitting we are powerless, is acknowledging that our spiritual life isn't about achieving some perfect state, but about living with things as they are.

As addicts I think we're especially susceptible to this kind of thinking. We want to control the world, for everything to be just so, and when it's not, we just throw up our hands and say, "Forget it. I don't care." One of the ways this is especially dangerous is when it's associated with a slip or relapse in our program. So often, it seems, when people do take a drink, a drug, or otherwise slip in whatever their program is, there's a sense of "Well, now that I slipped I might as well go whole hog," and they fall into a binge or abandon their program all together. For many people, relapse is actually part of the process of recovery, and is best viewed as a temporary setback. For an addict, in fact, it's quite normal, and to judge ourselves for such behavior is to not acknowledge the power of addiction and the challenge of recovery. Many people come back from relapse and are able to sustain longterm recovery. The most dangerous attitude is that relapse represents a personal and complete failure.

In the Step One exercise "Tracing Back Recovery," I pointed out the tendency to think that before recovery we were "bad," and now we are "good." This is another example of the extremes of addict thinking. We want to look at the world in terms of black and white, but that overlooks the subtle shadings of reality. This too is all or nothing thinking.

* **The Flaw of Memory**

On retreat our whole job, in a sense, is to look closely at our own minds. One of the things that I've noticed is that when a thought comes, like remembering an old girlfriend, I might start thinking about all my old girlfriends; or, I'll be walking in the woods, and I'll start thinking about the woods near where I grew up; or when I see that dinner is lasagna, I'll think of the restaurant where I get lasagna.

You get the idea: present moment thoughts and perceptions trigger memories. The reason for this is that our minds want to put what we are experiencing in this moment into a context. We want to see if there is anything from our past that can help us to deal with the present moment situation. This is particularly true of situations that our mind perceives as dangerous. This makes sense from an evolutionary perspective. If your mother was eaten by a saber-toothed tiger, it's good if you remember that and try to avoid them in the future.

However, when this kind of thinking pervades our mind without awareness, it can trigger some negative consequences. For instance, when I start to feel depressed, I remember all the times I've been depressed, and I can't remember not being depressed. That creates the sense in me that I am *always depressed*. This is the flaw of memory.

When we have a painful interaction with someone, we remember our past painful interactions and think, "I'm always having these kinds of interactions."

When we are anxious, we remember being anxious; when angry, we remember anger; when happy, we remember being happy. And so on. We can wind up with a totally unbalanced view of ourselves and our lives.

The result of this memory flaw can be many of the traditional cognitive distortions:

- Filtering – seeing only one side of things, usually negative.
- Mistaken assumptions – one small detail or event convinces us that someone hates us or some bad thing. is going to happen.
- Blowing out of proportion – everything else fades into the background as the one thing that obsesses us takes over our mind.

In your own meditation, if you watch closely and really consider what your thoughts are saying, I bet you'll discover other "cognitive distortions."

Meditation: Mindfulness of Mind

In order to do this practice you should first become somewhat familiar with the list of cognitive distortions, as well as the general concept of these misleading thoughts.

Begin your meditation in the usual way, settling into your posture, relaxing, and placing the attention on the breath. Once you have been sitting with the breath for a few minutes, begin to notice the thoughts that arise. Each time you become aware that you are thinking, notice if the thought falls into one of the categories of cognitive distortions. Don't try to do anything with the thought—judge it, analyze it, or figure out where it came from. Just notice the type of distortion and then return to the breath.

Outside of your meditation period you might look further into these thoughts, but when meditating, keep the process very simple: notice the thought and return to the breath. As you begin to see your biased thinking, one thought after another, your relationship to these thoughts naturally changes. You don't have to do anything, because this sort of repetition will undermine your belief in such thoughts. Trust the process of mindfully observing.

Step Eleven

"Sought through prayer and meditation to improve our conscious contact with God as we understood Him, praying only for knowledge of his will for us and the power to carry that out."

What's This Step About?

Step Eleven is probably the Step that people with a Buddhist orientation will be drawn to first when they see the Steps. I know I was. In fact, seeing the word "meditation" in the Steps was one of the things that made it comfortable to hang around 12 Step meetings when I was still skeptical of the whole process.

Step Eleven is also one of the main reasons that people read my books and come to my retreats and workshops. The Twelve Step literature doesn't give much guidance for meditation, and of course Buddhism is one of the best know meditation traditions, so it's natural that people in recovery would seek it out.

But of course the Step doesn't just say "meditate." It's more complicated than that, saying that we should meditate (and pray) for a particular purpose, to get closer to God and gain knowledge of what God wants us to do and for "Him" to help us to take those actions. When taken literally, I simply can't relate to this whole concept, mainly because it implies that God is some kind of being (a male, by the way) who has some kind of plan for me or preference for my behavior. While I know that many people believe in this sort of God, I don't, and so I've had to interpret this Step for myself, and of course, the way I do that is by trying to view the whole process through a Buddhist lens.

I've tried to describe this process in both my previous books, so you might take a look at *One Breath at a Time* and *A Burning Desire* to get more perspective. Here are some of my key ideas:

- "Conscious contact" is essentially what mindfulness is, a clear, present-moment connection to what is real right now.
- "God" or "Higher Power" can be seen as the Dharma, especially the Law of Karma, the Eightfold Path (including mindfulness), Lovingkindness, and the Three Characteristics of Existence: impermanence, suffering, and not-self.
- Prayer can be seen as a setting of intention and a reminder of how we want to live in the world.
- The "will of God" is the same thing as the goal of the Buddhist path, freedom from suffering. Our mindfulness practice makes us more sensitive to how we create suffering for ourselves and others. By responding to what we learn in meditation and in our daily mindfulness, we are acting to move toward this freedom.
- Power comes from each element of the Buddhist path: mindfulness is powerful; morality is powerful; wisdom is powerful. Love, faith, and forgiveness are powerful. Speech, livelihood, intention; concentration, effort, compassion. All of these are powers. Letting go is powerful.

What Is Meditation?

Stephen Batchelor, the brilliant and iconoclastic Buddhist teacher talks in his book *The Faith to Doubt* of our tendency to try to turn meditation into a mechanical process: "Symptomatic of the prevailing obsession with calculation, [meditation] is considered as a *technique*, as a systematic application of a preconceived series of ideas." People come to meditation thinking they'll learn this technique and get the results they want, whether less stress, a spiritual experience, or freedom from pain. Our culture is very results oriented, so we figure, if we're going to put in our time (and maybe pay some money) we should get some tangible result. And, of course, that result should come right away.

Anyone who has even a passing familiarity with what happens when you meditate knows that such an expectation is not only going to be frustrated, but will in fact undermine the very process of meditation.

Meditation isn't a technique that we learn so that we can control something—our minds, our bodies, our emotions, or our spiritual state. Meditation is a letting go of control, stepping into a timeless human process that unfolds in its own arc, in its own way. We are just passengers on this trip, we're not steering the boat. This fact can be very difficult for people to accept, which is why so many of the questions people have about meditation boil down to "How can I control what's happening?":

"How can I stop my thoughts?"

"How can I keep from falling asleep?"

"How can I make my knees stop hurting?"

Even, "How can I get enlightened?" These are all the wrong questions. The only real question in mindfulness meditation is "What is happening right now?"

Step Eleven is pointing to this same idea, albeit in a much more theistic way. When it says "praying only for knowledge of His will for us and the power to carry that out," it's saying that this process isn't about our agenda. It's about something else, about connecting with something beyond our personal (and perhaps petty) concerns. What all of the great religious and spiritual traditions point to is that none of this work is about "me." Buddhism points us toward compassion and service; the 12 Steps end with the admonition to "carry the message" to others who suffer; the whole Abrahamic tradition (Judaism, Christianity, and Islam) fosters love and service. The paradox of this teaching is that true personal happiness comes from letting go of our personal agenda and trying to serve others—or in religious language, to serve God.

This shift, then, from approaching meditation with personal goals, to letting a process play out in its own way and its own time, is key to practice. Meditation is a mysterious experience; it reveals aspects of ourselves and of reality that often lay hidden; it can take us to realms of mind beyond comprehension; and it can bring a sense of aliveness unsurpassed in human experience. But we can't discover any of this by rote practice or mechanics. Our heart/mind runs on its own schedule and its own logic. From a Buddhist viewpoint, our role is to observe this process; from a more devotional view, we might say our role is to honor, love, and surrender to this process, which can be called "the will of God."

How Does Meditation Work?

Stephen Batchelor, after disparaging the effort to turn meditation into another technique, tells us what he thinks it really is: "A meditative attitude is nothing new or alien. It dwells deeply within us all. . . It is not something that we have to bring from elsewhere and introduce into our lives. It is already present in an embryonic and sporadic way." We don't have to import mindfulness or peace; they live within us, waiting to be awakened. All the techniques of meditation, whether mantra or breath, lovingkindness or body scan, are simply ways to open us to these already existing aspects of ourselves. In fact, one of my, perhaps silly, theories is that all these techniques are simply ways to get us to sit still long enough for the actual process to unfold. So often I've found that after a long period of pretty much failing to be mindful or concentrated, mindfulness and concentration just seemed to arrive.

In the 12 Step world we say that we should "suit up and show up" because so much of our behavior before recovery was irresponsible. We find in recovery that if we just show up for our responsibilities, even if we don't feel like it or don't think there's any point, good things often happen. This connects to the Third Step idea of turning things over, doing our part and trusting "God" to supply the results. I've found that applying this same principle to meditation is highly effective. Rather than setting out goals or trying to control my experience, if I just show up day after day on my meditation cushion, if I just keep going on retreats and following the schedule, if I just keep trying to be mindful in my daily life, everything unfolds in its own time and in truly wonderful ways. It's not easy to do this; this unfolding can take years and run us through some very difficult and painful gauntlets. But I've found no real alternative. Trying to control my meditation and my spiritual growth is just a prescription for frustration. That frustration can lead to giving up, the one irredeemable crime of spiritual life—and, indeed, of recovery.

Of course, what I'm talking about is the same as the process of recovery. We can't control our growth in recovery; we just have to show up and do our best. We'll likely go through a lot of struggles and pain, and the timeframe for all of that is completely out of our hands. The result of sustained recovery, though, is almost invariably good. And, after all, what is the alternative? It was our efforts to control everything that got us into trouble as addicts in the first place.

So, ultimately, we see once again that the path is about letting go. Letting go in meditation, letting go in recovery.

Techniques of Meditation

Despite what I've said about not turning meditation into just a technique, I've offered many meditation practices in this book. This isn't to suggest that these techniques bring some guaranteed result, but rather that they give us tools for developing what Batchelor calls a "meditative attitude," that natural state of peace and presence. When talking about meditation techniques the Buddha used the metaphor of a raft, that we use the raft to cross the flood of samsara, but having arrived on the opposite shore, we don't continue to carry it. We need to see the techniques for what they are, tools to be used and let go of, not jewels to be clung to.

Here I'll add a few more techniques, some of my personal favorites and some that might require more experience than the introductory practices.

Meditation: The Golden Light

I learned this practice from Ayya Khema in her book *When the Iron Eagle Flies*. It is a form of *metta* or lovingkindness meditation that uses visualization. You can memorize these instructions, record them, or have someone read them slowly. The meditation should take about 20 minutes, but you can do a shorter version if you don't have time.

Begin by bringing your attention to the middle of your chest, to the place called the "heart center." Feel your breath in the chest, in the heart. Relax and settle into your body.

Now imagine that in your heart there is a beautiful white lotus flower with its petals closed. Gradually, as you breathe, the petals peel back, and a golden light shines forth. Feel the golden light shining from the center of your heart.

Let the golden light radiate out and shine on a beloved person. See and feel them being filled with warmth, kindness, and love from the golden light.

Now your beloved reflects the golden light of love back to you, filling you with warmth, kindness, and love. Let your body be suffused with the light of love.

Now let the golden light radiate out to all those you care for, family and friends. See them, one by one, being filled with the light of love radiating from your heart.

Bring to mind neighbors, colleagues, and other "neutral" people, such as people you encounter in shops and cafes. Let the golden light radiate out to them, filling them with warmth, kindness, and love.

Bring to mind a difficult person, someone with whom you've had a conflict or resentment. It doesn't have to be the *most* difficult person.

Let the golden light radiate out to them, filling them with warmth, kindness, and love.

Now begin to radiate the golden light out in all directions, touching everyone in the room; in the building; in the neighborhood. Let the golden light spread throughout your town, touching all the beings, human, animals, birds, and insects.

Let the golden light spread further, across the land and across the sea. All beings are filled with the golden light.

Now the light surrounds and permeates the planet, touching all beings and all things. The earth itself infused with the golden light of lovingkindness.

And now let the golden light radiate out into space in all directions. Limitless, unbounded, filling all beings and all things. The entire universe filled with the golden light of lovingkindess, radiant, illuminated.

And now, coming back. Coming back to this room, to this body, this heart, to this breath. Bring the golden light back into your heart and let the lotus petals close over it again. See that this limitless lovingkindness lives in your own heart, is always there, available to you if you just open to it.

Meditation: Building Concentration

For many people, developing concentration is one of the biggest hurdles in meditation practice. The tool of mindfulness helps us to develop insight, but without concentration, the meditative experience itself can be frustrating, as the mind flits from place to place and the body struggles for comfort. Concentration helps us to hold the mind steady and to relax into the body.

The essence of concentration is called "one-pointedness." This term is often misunderstood. It doesn't mean that the attention is narrowed down to a tiny "point." It simply means that the mind stays focused on only one thing. That "thing" can be quite broad and spacious, or it can have a quality of movement, like the breath.

The way to achieve one-pointedness is to choose one "object" to pay attention to, and then, continuously bring the mind to that object. If the mind wanders, don't pay attention to where you've been or get caught in analysis or judgment, just come back and try to remain as long as possible with the object. If things are happening in the background of your experience, just let them be.

Note: Stillness of the body supports stillness of the mind. During the concentration exercises, try to remain perfectly still. Notice the subtle body movements that happen beneath your awareness.

Another note: You may not want to do these exercises for the full period of meditation. Try using a concentration practice for the first 5-10 minutes, then going back to mindfulness practice.

This comes from Thich Nhat Hanh, the Vietnamese Zen master in his book *Present Moment, Wonderful Moment.* It uses a set of phrases or verses called "Gathas."

GATHAS

Repeat the following phrases silently in unison with the breath, continuing to feel the physical sensations of the breath. Each pair of words or phrases corresponds to an inhalation and exhalation:

In breath - Out breath
Deep - Slow
Calm - Ease
Smile – Release
Present Moment - Wonderful Moment

If you lose track of which phrase you're on, simply start at the beginning again. As you repeat the phrases, also try to continue to feel the breath, either at the nostrils or the belly.

Try adopting the meaning of the words to your breathing and your experience if that feels comfortable. Letting the breath get deep and slow; becoming calm and easeful; allowing a slight smile to come to your lips; realizing the uniqueness of right now. Only do this if it feels right; it's not necessary to do it to achieve the benefits of the practice. Simply bringing the mind back to the phrases and the breath over and over will develop one-pointedness.

Meditation: Opening to Space

This practice works best when the mind is already settled, especially during or right after an intensive meditation retreat. Nonetheless, it's worth experimenting with. Some people will feel an affinity for this perspective, while others may find it too vague or just not something they connect with.

Start by doing some conscious relaxation.

Relax the muscles in the face. Let the jaw be relaxed. Relax the small muscles around the eyes. The forehead.

Move the attention down to the shoulders. Let the shoulders relax. The arms and hands.

Feel any sensations that appear, then move on.

Soften the belly so the breath can move deeply into the body. Let the chest be open, receptive.

Relax through the hips and pelvis. The legs and feet.

Now feel the whole body sitting. Feel the body as a single object. Notice how in that single object there are many different sensations happening at once.

Now open to sound. Notice any sounds you can hear. Sounds in the room. Sounds coming from outside. Sounds inside your own body.

Notice the spatial quality of sounds, where they are happening in your awareness. Notice that the sensations in the body seem closer than sounds outside. See that there is a field of awareness that has a spatial quality. Things we sense appear in different parts of the field, some near, some far; some left, some right. Just as when we listen to a stereo recording, there is a spectrum in which sounds and sensations appear.

Now notice that the breath is at the center of this spectrum or field. Be aware of the breath in this larger field or space of awareness. Be aware of the breath and the space.

Sit in the center of the space of mind.

Thoughts appear; sounds; sensations. Emotions arise. All in the space of mind.

If you get caught up in thinking, when you notice that, come back to the breath and the space. Relax again. Open to the spacious quality of your own awareness. Rest in that space.

Buddhist Prayer

Buddhist teachings on emptiness say that prayer, which is an expression of dualism, me praying to other, undermines absolute truth. However, many teachers say that the absolute and the relative must be balanced in our lives if we are to function in practical ways while living with a spiritual perspective on our experience. For addicts, who tend towards extremes, this view, that we must be responsible in our daily lives while not forgetting the bigger picture, is an important teaching that keeps us from losing our way. From this point of view, prayer can help to ground us in reality and form when our practice and program are becoming vague and undefined.

The Western view of Buddhism seems to be that Buddhists can't pray because they don't believe in God. This overlooks the fact many Asian Buddhists pray in much the same way as Western monotheists. In fact, authentic prayer can have many of the same effects and benefits as meditation. The line between the two isn't nearly as distinct as might be supposed.

Some Buddhist practices, such as lovingkindness meditation, are essentially prayers. Here we repeat phrases in order to cultivate certain feelings and attitudes and to bring peace to the heart and stillness to the mind. That sounds like it could be a definition of prayer. Certainly Christian mystics have historically used repetitive prayer for these purposes. The most obvious distinction between a Christian prayer and a Buddhist one is that the Christian prayer is directed to God, and Buddhist prayers are usually not directed to anyone. In this way, a Christian begins the Serenity Prayer by saying, "God, grant me the serenity. . . " while a Buddhist might change the phrasing to, "May I have the serenity. . . " Certainly different, but not radically so.

In my book *A Burning Desire* I made up prayers to go with each of the Higher Powers I defined. Many of these take the form of "intention setting" that echo Step Three, such as "I turn my will and my life over to the Higher Power of Karma. I vow to live in harmony with the moral laws of the universe and to use the power of Karma to support my spiritual and worldly growth."

This kind of statement, this kind of prayer, when repeated on a regular basis becomes a habituated way of viewing the world and our experiences. While we can think of mindfulness as a more open process of simply seeing suffering and its cause and naturally letting go, prayer such as this is more assertive, a statement of Right View that we wish to deepen and make a part of our psyche. In this way, we begin to respond to life differently, less from the self-centered view and more from a place of wisdom, love, and acceptance. Fundamentally, this is what I believe the purpose of prayer is.

Exercise: Prayers to Dharma God

This set of prayers comes from my book *A Burning Desire: Dharma God and the Path of Recovery*. They were my attempt to find a way to "speak" to a Buddhist Higher Power, taking an aspect of the Dharma, viewing it as a power, and then thinking about how I could "turn my will and my life over" to such a power.

I suggest that you see if one or two of these resonate deeply for you, and that you adopt those as part of your daily practice and program.

Karma:

I turn my will and my life over to the Higher Power of Karma. I vow to live in harmony with the moral laws of the universe and to use the power of Karma to support my spiritual and worldly growth.

Mindfulness:

I set my intention to be mindful today. I will try to stay in my body; I will try to let go of greedy and hateful thoughts; I will be present and open to my feelings; I will be awake to the needs of those around me.

Impermanence:

I turn my will and my life over to the Higher Power of Impermanence, embracing each moment and letting it go. I open myself to transformation and to the unknown. Recognizing that everything is in the process of perpetual change, I let go of my clinging to mind states, objects, and other beings.

Suffering:

I open myself to the Higher Power of Suffering, letting go of resistance and allowing its truth and power to guide me. I recognize that suffering is not personal, but shared by all beings, and I offer compassion and love to myself and all beings everywhere.

Not Self:

I open myself to the flow of personality, without attachment or aversion. May I be free from clinging to limiting ideas of who I am and open to changing and growing in ways that will serve me and all beings.

Love:

I open my heart to love. I vow to cultivate generosity and unconditional lovingkindness for all beings. I seek to abandon hatred and meet anger with compassion.

Right View:

I commit my heart and mind to the search for truth, to seeing the Dharma in all things. May I be free from ignorance.

Right Intention:

I open my heart to the wisdom and power of my highest intention. May I stay attuned to and follow it always.

Right Speech:

I vow to refrain from the use of false or harmful speech and to speak with love and wisdom; may my words bring harmony and freedom.

Right Action:

Just for today, I vow to follow the Five Precepts, living with kindness and clarity. May my actions be of benefit to all beings.

Right Livelihood:

I vow to devote my livelihood to service, for others and myself. May those efforts enrich my life and that of all beings.

Right Effort:

May I find a balance of mind in practice, neither struggling nor halting. May I have the wisdom and strength to cultivate the good and abandon the harmful.

Right Concentration:

I commit myself to staying focused and allowing concentration to grow. I trust that if I am still and come back to the breath, serenity will deepen.

Faith:

May my heart be open, and may I trust myself and my path. May I surrender to the Twelve Steps and the Buddha's teachings, the Dharma. May I live in fearlessness, and may my faith inspire my efforts in my program and my practice.

Presence:

I open myself to the presence of God, and I trust that when I can't feel God, It is still here with me.

Spiritual Awakening:

May my efforts in practice bring spiritual awakening. May my awakening be of benefit to all beings.

Community:

I commit myself to being a part of my recovery and practice communities. I open myself to the wisdom of these groups and I offer myself in service to them.

Exercise: The Third Step Prayer

On page 63 of *Alcoholics Anonymous*, better known as *The Big Book*, a prayer is suggested for the Third Step. On one of my retreats a woman named Chris S. from New Hampshire offered her Buddhist version:

"I offer myself to the Three Jewels, to learn, live, and be changed by the Dharma. May the teachings be put into practice in my life and relieve my suffering and help to relieve the suffering of others. May the Power of the Dharma working in my life be a source of inspiration to others I may help of the Buddha's wisdom, the Dharma's truth, and the Sangha's strength. May I follow the path always."

The Lord's Prayer

Many 12 Step meetings close with the traditional Christian "Lord's Prayer," or as I knew it growing up, the "Our Father." If you aren't Christian or don't believe in God, it can be difficult to hear this prayer. In my book, *One Breath at a Time: Buddhism and the Twelve Steps*, I did a bit of a gloss on the Lord's Prayer to show a more Buddhist way of understanding it. Here is an update of that piece:

"Our Father who art in Heaven..."

As I say this part of the prayer I have a sense of opening to something larger than my limited sense of self. It's a kind of surrender. I can also have the sense of addressing my highest self, the place in me that is wise, patient, peaceful, loving, and compassionate—Heaven. So, I'm beginning the prayer by calling on my best qualities.

"Hallowed be thy name..."

When Buddhists pay homage to the Buddha, they seem to be doing something like this, bowing out of respect. As I say this, I'm invoking the spiritual aspect of life, of all that is. There's a sense of humility being evoked here, too, which Bill Wilson says is "the foundation principle" of the Steps.

"Thy Kingdom come, thy will be done, on earth as it is in Heaven."

Here, as I say the prayer, I imagine my highest wisdom coming down into the nitty-gritty details of my life, down to earth, with the Kingdom of Heaven--that is, the place of purity and wisdom in me-- becoming manifest through thought, word, and deed. "Thy will," refers to Right Intention, acting from the desire to be of service to all beings.

"Give us this day our daily bread..."

I understand this as an appreciation of interdependence, recognizing that the whole universe is supporting my existence: the atmosphere for air, the earth for food and water, and everything else that allows me to live in this moment. In that sense, it's a recognition of powerlessness; if not for the bounty of the universe, I wouldn't even be alive.

"Forgive us our trespasses as we forgive those who trespass against us..."

Obviously this echoes the Golden Rule, treating others as we would like to be treated. The recognition of our own imperfection is vital to accepting the imperfection of others, and for a meditator, the moment-to-moment forgiveness as we fall off the meditation object and into wandering thoughts is vital to settling in, to allowing the process to unfold naturally. If we are judging—not forgiving—ourselves each time we space out or forget to pay attention, we only create more suffering. So, we set our intention here to be kind and accepting of ourselves and our failures.

"Lead us not into temptation, but deliver us from evil."

For an addict or alcoholic, these words are important—and point to something real. In practical terms, we need to avoid situations and people that might trigger relapse; you don't hang out in bars if you don't have business there, and you don't drop by your drug dealer's house for a social call. In Buddhist terms, this is the aspect of Right Effort called prevention, where we try to keep negative thoughts or emotions from even appearing. The Buddha, knowing the tendencies of the mind to veer into desire and aversion, encouraged quite strong effort to counter these destructive habits. So, although I resist the Biblical language of "temptation" and "evil," the meaning beneath the words is relevant--if you can just let go of the judgment.

For a former Catholic like me, this is where the prayer ends, but in Twelve Step meetings, the Protestant version continues with a final turning over of "for thine is the Kingdom, the Power, and the Glory," which affirms our intention to surrender to the highest truth.

Step Twelve

"Having had a spiritual awakening as the results of these Steps, we tried to carry this message to others [with our addiction], and to practice these principles in all our affairs."

What's This Step About?

Step Twelve has three components: spiritual awakening, carrying the message, and practicing the principles. I'll address each of these components separately, but let me encapsulate here. The thrust, as I understand the Step, is that, while we've been transformed by our Step work, the higher purpose of our recovery is to be of service to others who suffer in the same ways we did, and that, in order to fulfill the work of recovery, we must bring our spiritual values into every facet of our lives in an ongoing way.

The traditional Twelve Step understanding is that "we can't keep it if we don't give it away." The founders of AA discovered that it was only when they set out to help other alcoholics that they could sustain their own sobriety. They saw that focusing on the concerns of others got them out of their self-centeredness and was a great relief. Carrying the message then works both as service to others and protection for ourselves.

Spiritual Awakening

When I first went to a meeting and saw Step Twelve, I thought these alcoholics didn't know what they were talking about. Caught up in my confused Buddhist perspective on enlightenment, I thought "spiritual awakening" meant some kind of magical, mind-blowing mystical experience that turned you into a saint. The idea that you could follow the 12 Steps (of which I had no understanding) to get a spiritual awakening made no sense to me.

Today, that belief has been turned on its head.

First of all, I can see that there are many levels of spiritual awakening, up to and including what Buddhists call "full enlightenment." The different schools and traditions of Buddhism describe so many different versions of this that it's almost absurd to try to define it. In the Theravadan tradition this is equated with no longer being driven by desire and aversion, and no longer being attached to or believing in a separate self. The idea is that the things that cause inner turmoil and stress no longer affect you. The end of suffering.

I don't think that Step Twelve is claiming this kind of ultimate freedom, but that doesn't mean that the spiritual awakening of recovery isn't powerful and transformative. In fact, since recovery is largely about learning to not act on desire and aversion, as well as becoming less self-centered, in many ways it does parallel this definition of enlightenment, if not to the full extent.

Today I see Step One as the most powerful transformative experience of my life. Simply seeing that I could no longer use drugs and alcohol and then stopping changed everything. I awoke to the destructive power of drugs and alcohol in my life and to the potential of living clean and sober. Taking that Step opened the door for the radical transformation of my life. At that time I was 35 years old and my material life was in shambles, no car, no insurance, an empty bank account, and barely employed. I was a high school dropout who'd been relying on drugs and alcohol for nineteen years. I'd been through a series of failed relationships. I'd been living with untreated depression for decades. Nothing had really changed either internally or externally since my early twenties.

By fully taking that first Step, a dozen years later I had a master's degree in creative writing, I was engaged to be married, and I was in a Buddhist teacher-training program. I'd learned to manage depression. And I never even thought about drinking. Everything had changed.

The reason I describe all these changes is that when we talk about spiritual awakening it can seem somewhat esoteric. We can have big spiritual insights, but that doesn't mean our lives will change. You can go on a meditation retreat (as I did before getting sober) and think that you've figured it all out. But if you don't start to live differently, it's won't really matter. You can read a Buddhist book and think that you understand it, but if you don't change inside, what's the real value?

Spiritual awakening isn't just a *seeing*, but also a *doing*. And that's what the 12 Steps focus on, living differently. We begin by stopping our addictive behaviors, but that's just the beginning. Recovery involves a deep and careful examination of ourselves, our lives, our behaviors, our prejudices, our preferences, all of it, so that we can see what needs to change. It means trying to heal the inner wounds while behaving with wisdom and compassion even when we don't feel like it.

And, of course, Step One isn't the only spiritual awakening. In fact, I think we can see each of the Steps as an awakening. Here are some examples of those awakenings:

- Step Two awakens us to the possibility of change
- Step Three awakens us to commitment and acceptance
- Step Four awakens us to our own failings
- Step Five awakens us to the power of confession
- Step Six awakens us to the power of intention
- Step Seven awakens us to the power of letting go
- Step Eight awakens us to the truth of who we harmed
- Step Nine awakens us to the power of forgiveness
- Step Ten awakens us to the importance of enduring effort
- Step Eleven awakens us to our inner goodness and spiritual life
- Step Twelve awakens us to service and commitment

Exercise: Spiritual Awakening

What is spiritual awakening for you? Reflect first on the meaning of "spiritual." Then consider how you understand the term, "spiritual awakening." Finally, reflect on the ways that you have awakened spiritually.

Carrying the Message

The ancient texts say that when the Buddha achieved enlightenment, he thought that this breakthrough was so rarified that no one would be able to understand it. He wondered if trying to teach people about his path would just be frustrating and disappointing. However, in the mythology of these teachings, it's said that he was visited by a god who told him, "There are some with just a little dust in their eyes," and that he should teach out of compassion for all the beings who suffer.

Step 12 tells us something very similar: that our spiritual awakening isn't just for our own sake, that it must be shared with others for it to have real value. This reflects another parallel between the Step and Buddhism: that our self-centeredness is the cause of our suffering, and that if, instead, we think about others, we'll be happier. Of course, from a Buddhist view, the very idea of a solid, lasting self is an illusion, so trying to find happiness through focusing on that illusion is obviously a losing battle. The Steps don't go this far, but the end result is much the same: we discover the joy of service.

Of course, like anything else, taking on the commitment to serve others has its risks. There are many people, for instance, who have been overly focused on others, and not enough on themselves. Programs like Co-Dependents Anonymous and Al-Anon specifically serve such people. For them, finding the balance between self-care and care for others may be the first task in the process of recovery. But that doesn't mean they won't want to carry the message.

In fact, anyone who tries to fulfill this Step will be faced with the challenge of trying to help others without being attached to the results. Not being attached to the results of *any* action is one of the great challenges of spiritual practice, and here that becomes even more evident. Trying to help alcoholics and addicts of any stripe is tricky. When I got to this Step with my sponsor at two years sober, he suggested I start to offer to sponsor others with less clean time than me. The first person I worked with was on probation, and when he slipped on cocaine and got a dirty drug test, wound up back in jail, in a maximum-security prison in Southern California. I visited him there. Seeing what had happened to him, I felt like a failure, but that was really just the beginning of my realization that I couldn't control

Kevin Griffin

others, and that I wasn't responsible for their behavior. It's hard enough for me to control *myself*, how can I expect to control other people?

So, service isn't about controlling people or about results. It's about getting out of ourselves and letting go. The logic of it is simple: if I'm thinking about others, I'm not thinking about myself; if I'm doing good things for people, I feel good about myself.

Twelve Step programs provide easy ways to dip your toe into service by taking a commitment at a meeting. You can be a secretary or treasurer, make coffee or take care of literature. This is a great way for someone who has never done a lot for others (like me when I got sober) to discover how good it feels to contribute to your community. The bigger step is sponsorship, whereby one person helps another to work the Steps, and to generally navigate the challenging seas of early recovery. Indeed, many people continue to work with a sponsor long after early recovery. So the program makes service a central part of 12 Step life.

But, to view service as strictly about "carrying the message to other" addicts like us is to have a fairly narrow understanding of the possibilities of this aspect of our spiritual lives. All spiritual and religious traditions promote service and generosity as critical values, and for a person in recovery, expanding our sense of service just opens up the possibilities. Certainly our world has many opportunities for direct service, especially in communities where poverty and illness are common. Schools offer another opportunity, as so many are underfunded. If we are looking for a chance to help, there are many organizations that need volunteers.

But service doesn't just mean this sort of formal commitment. Service, once again, is about intention, and if we bring a spirit of service to our lives, we'll find opportunities everywhere we look. We don't have to see service as anything special or anything more than wanting to be helpful to a friend, relative, or neighbor. If we bring a spirit of service to our work, we may find that there is greater inspiration in what we do.

More than doing particular "good works," I think that our intention to live a life that brings benefit to our family, our community, our business, and our world will create positive results. We don't have to run out and become do-gooders all of a sudden. We just have to keep our eyes and hearts open to opportunities, big and small.

Exercise: Am I Helping?

This exercise is meant to help you see how you are already being of service and how you might be of more service. Consider how you bring both the intention and the actions of service to these aspects of your life:

- **Family**: Do you try to help older family members? Younger ones? Your partner? Are you doing enough? Too much? If you don't feel you are doing enough, begin to look for more ways to help family members. If you feel you are doing too much, try to practice saying "No" to your family.
- **Friends**: Are you of service to your friends? When they ask for help, are you there? Do you do enough for them? Too much? If you don't feel you are doing enough, begin to look for more ways to help your friends. If you feel you are doing too much, try to practice saying "No" to your friends.
- **Work**: Do you act with a spirit of service at your work or do you just put in your time and collect a paycheck? What would happen

if you viewed your work as more than a living, but an opportunity to be of service? Are you helpful enough at work? Too helpful? If you don't feel you are doing enough, begin to look for more ways to help at work. If you feel you are doing too much, try to practice saying "No" to your boss.

- **Program**: Are you contributing to your program? Are you doing enough? Too much? If you don't feel you are doing enough, begin to look for more ways to help in your program. If you feel you are doing too much, try to practice saying "No" to people in the program.

- **Spiritual community**: Are you doing service for your spiritual community? Are you doing enough? Too much? If you don't feel you are doing enough, begin to look for more ways to help your spiritual community. If you feel you are doing too much, try to practice saying "No" to people in your spiritual community (including teachers).

In All Our Affairs

"Practiced these principles in all our affairs" closes all the loopholes. There's no time when we are "off duty" in a spiritual practice. This is the way we live now. In the same way that we can't take a day off from our recovery without bearing serious consequences, if we slip on our spiritual values and principles we undermine our integrity, self-esteem, and relationships, both personal and professional.

From the Buddhist viewpoint, maintaining mindfulness in "all our affairs" is key. While mindfulness meditation is invaluable, perhaps the greater challenge is to bring mindfulness more thoroughly into our daily lives. This consistent attention will change our behavior and our inner life. If we are paying attention, we can't help but be more compassionate, thoughtful, and wise. When we see the results of our actions, we naturally act more skillfully, more in harmony with karma. When we are present we see the Dharma in all things; when we see the Dharma in all things, we naturally let go.

These are our goals, but it's important that we remember to be patient, compassionate and forgiving of ourselves as we'll inevitably make mistakes or lose our way.

Having some sense of what the principles of Buddhism and recovery are can help to guide us. Here is one version of traditional 12 Step principles:

- Step One – Honesty
- Step Two – Hope
- Step Three – Faith
- Step Four – Courage
- Step Five – Integrity
- Step Six – Willingness
- Step Seven – Humility
- Step Eight – Brotherly/Sisterly Love
- Step Nine - Justice
- Step Ten - Perseverance
- Step Eleven - Spirituality
- Step Twelve – Service

And here are some key Buddhist principles:

- Mindfulness
- Trust in Karma
- Taking Refuge
- Investigation

- Sangha (Community)
- Right Intention
- Letting Go
- Forgiveness
- Long Enduring Mind (Patience)
- Samadhi (Concentration)
- Compassion

Finally, here are a few principles shared by Buddhism and the 12 Steps:

- Awareness is the underpinning to recovery and personal growth.
- Clinging causes suffering; letting go brings freedom and happiness.
- It's seeing our own suffering clearly that inspires us to change and let go.
- Surrender to powers greater than ourselves reflects wisdom and humility. Without surrender, ego dominates and limits our growth.
- Change only happens with willingness.
- "Take what you need and leave the rest." Use whatever tools are available. This is the Buddhist principle of *"upaya"* or "skillful means." We're not interested in ideology but in results.

Exercise: Your Principles

While it's useful to see and try to follow principles laid down by others, what's more important is for us to know what the principles that guide us are. For this exercise make a list or share the principles you want to live by.

Appendix A: Buddhist Recovery Meetings

This appendix contains suggestions for starting a Buddhist recovery meeting, a suggestion of a preamble for such meetings, and a prayer I use to close meetings.

Group Guidelines

Buddhist recovery meetings are a kind of hybrid meditation/12 Step form, with more meditation than a typical 12 Step meeting and more sharing than a typical meditation group. Some are led by a teacher, others by peers.

Here are some guidelines for starting a group, covering these topics:

- Intention
- Leadership
- Membership
- Form and Content

Intention

Setting a clear intention is the vital starting point for someone thinking about forming a group. Is your main focus going to be in deepening your Step work? deepening your meditation practice? dharma study? forming community and giving a place to share? Answering these and other questions about what you want from your group will help you to decide on the other questions of leadership, membership, form, and content. For instance, if your main interest is in growing the community, you might want open membership, whereas, if you want to focus on deepening meditation and forming intimate connections, you might want a closed membership.

What might be more critical in thinking about intention is in distinguishing the purpose of a Buddhism/Twelve Step group from that of an ordinary Twelve Step group. What I always try to look for in any Buddhist discussion is, How does what we're talking about relate to the dharma? So, if someone is helping a sick relative, to put it in the context of the Buddha's teaching on suffering, that we are all subject to sickness, old age, and death. This doesn't mean that we deny people their need to process grief or any difficult emotions—on the contrary, being fully present with those painful experiences is vital to the process of moving through them and healing—but it does mean that at some point we remind ourselves of the context of our experience and don't stay stuck in the "story." This is a common difficulty in any group focused on spirituality and healing—it's so easy for us to stay in the "problem" and forget the solution. While it's helpful to talk about our difficulties, if we don't move beyond examining our pain toward looking at the Path of freedom, we miss the point of the spiritual teachings.

So, whoever is facilitating, be it a teacher or just a member of the group, this focus on intention should be kept very strong. In Twelve Step groups we call this "primary purpose" and in Buddhism "Right Intention."

Leadership

Leadership can be approached in two basic ways: set facilitators who organize and lead the group, or "group conscience" which is essentially a democracy. The advantage of having set facilitators is that they would be more experienced practitioners who could hold the group together more strongly. Some of the disadvantages are the potential for projection that a leader gets, where people in the group like or dislike things the leader says or does and the tendency for members to not take responsibility for the group, expecting the leader to do all the work. So this form opens the door for the "personalities before principles" issue that Twelve Step groups seek to avoid. The advantage of a more democratic form are that everyone feels fully invested in the group and takes their share of responsibility. The disadvantage can be that if there is no experienced practitioner, the group might find itself going down unproductive paths. Kalyana Mitta (KM) groups can devolve (as can Twelve Step groups) into little more than group therapy sessions, and, without a leader to guide the group back to its foundation principles, this can undercut the group goals. My preference, then, is for leadership, but I also know that the "benign anarchy" of Twelve Step groups can be very effective. What I think is most important in that case is that the group have a very strong intention—even a mission statement of some sort—so that it can always come back to its core purpose, in the same way that Twelve Step groups emphasize a "singleness of purpose."

When I led a KM group, I was asked to lead it by a senior teacher. This is the typical way that one takes a teaching or leadership role in the Buddhist community, through the aegis of an established teacher. One could say that Buddhism is hierarchical (which is true), but the hierarchy isn't supposed to be based so much on *power* as on *wisdom*. What this means is that a teacher or leader's authority grows out of their realization, out of the depth of their practice and their understanding, and not out of some personal "leadership qualities" which might make them popular or powerful, nor out of their own desire to be a leader. Traditionally the person who certifies this depth of practice is another, more senior, teacher. In this way, the Buddhist tradition has kept alive a "lineage" of enlightened (or at least wise and trustworthy) masters through two and a half millenia. It's a system that, although it doesn't fit so well with our culture's current concerns about consensus, democracy, and egalitarianism, has, nonetheless *worked*, and success like that, I believe, needs to be respected and at least considered as a legitimate criteria. After all, if our spiritual leaders were elected on the basis of their popularity we'd have teachers with great personalities, but perhaps not a lot of wisdom (like our political leaders?).

So, what I'd suggest is that if a group is forming around some leaders, that those leaders should be certified or supported in some way by more senior teachers. If they are taking a leadership role, then that suggests that they have a depth of practice, which in turn suggests that they have studied with a teacher or teachers who they could call on as support. Anyone in a leadership role in a spiritual community needs such mentoring and support—the difficulties and risks associated with these roles are too great to handle alone. Specifically, if you are thinking of starting a group, I suggest that you contact a teacher with whom you have studied and ask for their support and mentoring in your new role.

Typically, KM groups have two facilitators. This is a good idea for many reasons. (Check out http://www.spiritrock.org/html and select "Community" then "Dharma Friends" to find a discussion of KM groups).

If, on the other hand, a group decides to form without a leader, a different approach will be taken. What I would suggest is a revolving facilitator role, where at the end of each gathering, one or two people agree to be facilitators for the next meeting. The group could keep a list of guidelines which the facilitators would follow. Such guidelines should be simple, but specific so that the group meetings are consistent. This is essentially the *secretary* role that is held in most Twelve Step groups. This person keeps track of the time, stays sensitive to the needs of the group and the individuals in the group—for instance, making sure that one person doesn't dominate or that a quieter person doesn't get left out of the discussion. They lead the group through the session, ringing the bell for meditation, reminding people of the structure of the session, and so on. Structure and a sense of orderliness are important for allowing people to relax and feel safe in the group.

Membership

How should you determine membership? How many members should you have? Who decides who can join? Or should it be a drop-in group, like a Twelve Step group, which is totally open to anyone who is interested. All of these questions need to be addressed by the facilitators and/or the members. While some KM groups require a certain meditation practice experience (like two years or a ten-day retreat), for a Buddhism/Twelve Step group, this seems unwise, because such groups are going to be especially appealing to Twelve Steppers with little or no meditation experience who want support in their practice. So, my suggestion is that groups have no requirement for meditation experience. On the other hand, if what you want is a group of experienced meditators who are also sober (clean, abstinent) then by all means, set a practice requirement. What any group will want to do is suggest that members establish a daily (or as close to daily as possible) meditation practice.

Do you want to have a sobriety requirement? Again, this is a decision for your group and/or leaders to make. If you are a closed group, you might want to have a suggested sobriety length (six months or a year?) and then take other applications on a case-by-case basis. If someone is completely new to meditation, slipping a lot, and perhaps detoxing, they might not be great members of the group. However, your group might want to reach out to such people, in the same way Twelve Step groups welcome people so openly. The only problem is that the nature of a meditation group is one of more quiet and a bit more serenity than a typical Twelve Step meeting, and any disruption could really have an adverse effect. Another person might want to join who had previous meditation experience and is newly sober but seems stable in their recovery. They might be a welcome addition to the group.

Typically a KM group is closed, as opposed to drop-in. This allows for the development of community and closeness among the members and a feeling of safety and support. Buddhism/Twelve Step groups might want to consider this structure. However, you might feel that it's more important to be welcoming to the community than to keep the group closed. There are advantages and disadvantages to both.

Usually a KM group tries to maintain a range of membership, typically between 5 and 12. I'm not at all sure a Buddhism/Twelve Step group needs to stick to these relatively low numbers. Again, consider the pluses and minuses. It's amazing how intimate a Twelve Step group can be even when there are dozens of people there—still, there's no doubt that a smaller number allows for more of a sense of safety and support.

If you are starting a group, how will you attract members? If you're in a large urban area, you probably won't have much problem. You might even know a dozen people already, or at least by inviting a couple friends and seeing if they know anyone who might be interested, you might quickly fill the group. In a smaller area, or one in which Buddhist practitioners are more scarce, you might need to do some outreach. Clearly the first place to go is your Twelve Step meeting. If there's an Eleventh Step meeting in your area, that would be a likely starting point. You might also consider putting up a notice at a health food store or independent bookstore. Of course, the Internet gives us almost unlimited resources in terms of connecting with people.

Once the group is formed, you'll want to consider how new members are added. Can anyone in the group nominate someone or should everything go through the facilitators? In either case, any decision to confirm a new member should be contingent on their visiting the group and seeing how they fit in. Once someone's in, it's tough to get them out, so you don't want to make mistakes at this stage.

The KM model is obviously a restrictive one and one which Twelve Steppers used to the benign anarchy of meetings may find too rigid. In fact, I know of two very successful groups in the Bay Area which are completely open. They do have fairly strong leadership, but they don't seem to have any restrictions on membership. These groups tend to be full of energy and inspiration and are allowing people of all levels of sobriety and meditation experience to come together to form a strong community. My perspective as someone who is used to being the "teacher" and having more control over the setting probably biases me toward more restriction, but, the truth is that both models are completely valid and, again, the important question is, what do you want from your group? So, it comes down to intention. It's likely that a KM model will provide more opportunity for structured meditation practice, study, and development. The more 12 Step open model I think fosters more connection, service, and opportunity for new people. Ideally, it would be nice if both could be available to people.

Form and Content

Now we get to the meat of the group: what's going to happen when we get together? There probably aren't that many different things that a group will do: meditate, talk, read, socialize. It's just a matter of finding the form and content that is most helpful for your group.

In most meditation groups, the sitting, or meditation, period comes first. The reason for this may be that the meditation itself makes us more sensitive and open and allows us to both speak and listen with a clearer attention afterwards. It helps bring calm and stillness to the group and to give people a break from the busyness of their lives.

So, I recommend that once everyone is settled, that the group do some meditation. If you are an open group with drop-in members, it's probably best to give at least a little bit of meditation instruction. You can use the guided meditations in my books or any of a number of other books (see the booklist in Appendix B for some suggestions), or, if your leader is an experienced meditator, they might want to just give their own instructions.

Generally it's recommended that a meditation period be at least 20 minutes. For new people this might seem long, but it seems to be a widely accepted period. In fact, regular Buddhist meditation groups often sit for 45 minutes or even an hour. Obviously, each group will want to decide on the length of the meditation period.

Most groups end meditation with a bell. These can be purchased at spiritual bookstores, futon shops, meditation centers, health food stores, and online. A bell is a pleasant way to end a period of silence non-verbally. Some groups do chanting at the end of the meditation period, and, of course, a group might want to use a prayer, like the Serenity Prayer. In any case, it's nice to have a ritualized way of ending meditation. It allows for a smooth transition out of the silence.

After the meditation, depending on how long the meeting is going to last, you might want to have time to stretch and have tea. At most meditation groups the break is fairly short so that the quiet developed during the sitting doesn't dissipate too much, but for Buddhism/12 Step groups, the break is usually a more important part of the evening. This is when people get to connect informally which is very valuable.

Now you begin the interactive part of the session. If you are simply an open group, then you might just go right into sharing. A KM group often has a time for check-in where people talk about what's going on in their lives right now before going into a chosen topic. Or the leader/facilitator might want to begin by talking on a topic as a way of stimulating conversation and sharing some dharma understanding. Any of these models can be effective.

Some groups find it helpful to read some literature together, following the 12 Step "Book Study" model. If it's a KM group, you might suggest that people read a chapter of a book before the group meets so people can go right into discussion. A drop-in group might read aloud from the study book during the gathering. And, of course, a discussion would follow. Besides my two previous books, a couple that I think are suited for this kind of study are Jack Kornfield's *A Path with Heart*, Sharon Salzberg's *Lovingkindness*, and Pema Chodron's *When Things Fall Apart*. I'm sure members of your group will have their favorites as well.

Besides someone giving a talk, group sharing, reading, and discussion, a group might be interested in doing interactive exercises for working with specific Steps and concepts for bridging Buddhism and the Twelve Steps. Obviously, that's what this book is designed for.

For a KM group, it's helpful to have a "check-out" time where people can mention what was beneficial and what not so beneficial for them in the gathering. The facilitators can then adjust things according to people's needs.

It's nice to end any group with a blessing, prayer, or short lovingkindness (*metta*) meditation—less than five minutes. This puts a nice closing energy into the end of the session. One group I visited did both a "dedication of merit" and then got up and held hands to say the Serenity Prayer, just like a 12 Step meeting. That seems like a nice combination of the two.

Whatever of these suggestions you might adopt, I think you will find that a meditation group of any kind will be of great help to its members. When we practice together we strengthen our practice in a way that solitary meditation can't. The support and insight of others is invaluable in developing our practice. Everytime I join with a group to meditate my practice is inspired and energized. I wish you great joy, happiness, and awakening through your inner work.

Preamble

This piece is meant to accomplish the same purpose of the Preamble read at most 12 Step groups. Note that for peer led groups, the references to a teacher will be skipped.

"Welcome to the [name of group]. The purpose of this group is to support those who want to integrate Buddhist teachings and practices into their recovery from any addiction. We are open to people of all backgrounds and recovery paths, including, but not limited to all 12 Step programs. We encourage the use of mindfulness and meditation and are grounded in Buddhist principles of non-harming, compassion, and interdependence.

"While not affiliated with any 12-Step group, we do follow the 12-Step traditions of confidentiality and no cross talk between participants. (The teacher may comment on people's sharing.)

"While everyone is encouraged and welcome to share, this group is teacher-led. In the Buddhist tradition, teachers are trained and authorized by *their* teachers based on their practice and experience. They are expected to guide and facilitate their community members' practice."

[You might add:] "Before we begin the meditation period, please turn off your cell phones and any other electronic devices."

Closing Prayer

This is a prayer I adopted from a Buddhist teaching. It's usually done standing in a circle holding hands. Ordinarily I do it as a call-and-response, but if everyone in a group knew it, you could do it together.

Reflection on Sharing Blessings

May all beings receive the blessings of my life;

May I receive the blessings of my life;

May those I love receive the blessings of my life;

May those I do not love receive the blessings of my life;

May all beings receive the blessings of my life.

Keep coming back, it works!

Appendix B: Resources

Bibliography

Books mentioned in the text of *Buddhism & The Twelve Steps*

Introduction:

The Experience of Insight, by Joseph Goldstein

Mindfulness: A Practical Guide to Awakening, by Joseph Goldstein

For the Newcomer

Sober for Good, by Anne Fletcher

Step One

Alcoholics Anonymous (The Big Book)

Step Three

Twelve Steps and Twelve Traditions, by Bill W.

Step Four

Awakening Joy, by James Baraz

Step Six

Satipatthana: The Direct Path to Realization, by Analayo

Step Ten

Mindfulness-Based Cognitive Therapy, by by Williams, Seagal, et al

Feeling Good, by David Burns

Step Eleven

The Faith to Doubt, by Stephen Batchelor

When the Iron Eagle Flies, by Ayya Khema

Step Twelve

Present Moment, Wonderful Moment, by Thich Nhat Hanh

Other Recommended Reading

Mindfulness:

Wherever You Go, There You Are, by Jon Kabat-Zinn

Mindfulness-Based Stress Reduction, by Bob Stahl and Elisha Goldstein

Mindfulness in Plain English, by Bhante Gunaratana

Dharma:

A Path with Heart, by Jack Kornfield

The Experience of Insight, by Joseph Goldstein

Seeking the Heart of Wisdom, by Jack Kornfield and Joseph Goldstein

Who Is My Self?, by Ayya Khema

Buddhism Without Beliefs, by Stephen Batchelor

Lovingkindness, by Sharon Salzberg

Buddha's Nature, by Wes Nisker

Breath by Breath, by Larry Rosenberg

Sutta:

In the Buddha's Words, edited by Bhikkhu Bodhi

Majjhima Nikaya, translated by Bhikkhu Nanamoli and Bhikkhu Bodhi

Buddhist Recovery:

One Breath at a Time: Buddhism and the Twelve Steps, by Kevin Griffin

A Burning Desire: Dharma God and the Path of Recovery, by Kevin Griffin

Mindfulness and the Twelve Steps, by Therese Jacobs-Stewart

Chi Kung and Recovery, by Greg Pergament

Twelve Step:

Alcoholics Anonymous (The Big Book)

Twelve Steps and Twelve Traditions

Basic Text of Narcotics Anonymous

Others useful books:

At Hell's Gate: A Soldier's Journey from War to Peace, by Claude Anshin Thomas

Dharma Punx: A Spiritual Memoir, by Noah Levine

Waking the Tiger: Healing Trauma: The Innate Capacity to Transform Overwhelming Experiences, by Peter Levine

Wake Up: A Buddhist Guide for Teens, by Diana Winston

The Mindful Way through Depression, by Williams, Seagal, et al

Internet Resources

www.buddhistrecovery.org - The home of the Buddhist Recovery Network. Lists Buddhist Recovery meetings worldwide.

www.accesstoinsight.org - Theravadan Buddhist site with translations and commentary of the Pali Canon.

www.kevingriffin.net - my website.

www.spiritrock.org - Website for Spirit Rock Meditation Center in Northern California. Teachings offered in residential retreats, daylong retreats, and evening classes.

www.dharma.org - Website for three centers in Barre, MA: Insight Meditation Society (residential group retreats), Barre Center for Buddhist Studies (residential study retreats), and Forest Refuge (residential self-retreats).

www.amaravati.org - Website of Amaravati Monastery, the main monastery for Western monks in the Thai Forest Tradition.

Acknowledgments

This book was inspired by conversations with Jess O'Brien of New Harbinger Press and Stephanie Tate.

Thanks to my agent, Stephanie Tade who has guided my publishing life for many years.

Thanks to my wife, Rosemary Graham, always my biggest supporter

Thanks to my daughter, Graham Griffin for being a great daughter.

Thanks to all the people who have attended my workshops and retreats whose engagement has guided my teaching.

Thanks to the many dharma and spiritual centers that have supported my work.

Thanks to my teachers without whom I'd be wandering in the dark.

Thanks to the many friends in the 12 Step world who have supported my recovery.

Thanks to Chris S. for her version of the "Third Step Prayer."

Thanks to my friends Wes, Don, Roland, and Max who keep me honest.

CPSIA information can be obtained at www.ICGtesting.com
Printed in the USA
BVOW05s1949030516

446610BV00018B/375/P